WALKS INTO HISTORY
WARWICKSHIRE

John Wilks

COUNTRYSIDE BOOKS
3 Catherine Road
Newbury, Berkshire

To view our complete range of books,
please visit us at
www.countrysidebooks.co.uk

ISBN 978 1 84674 186 9

Designed by Peter Davies
Produced through MRM Associates Ltd., Reading
Typeset by CJWT Solutions, St Helens
Printed in Thailand

Contents

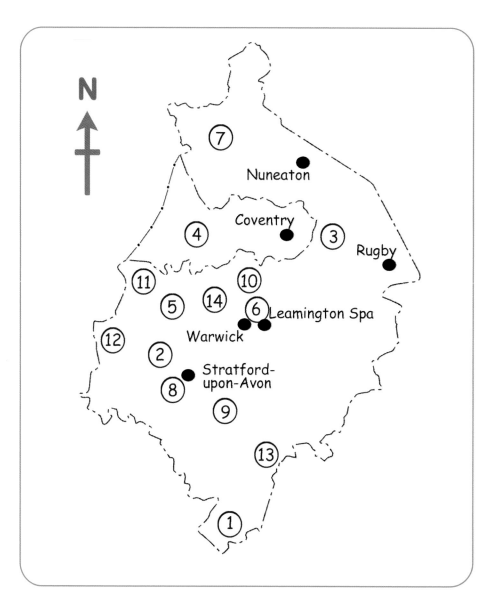

AREA MAP SHOWING LOCATION OF THE WALKS

WALK

PUBLISHER'S NOTE

We hope that you obtain considerable enjoyment from this book; great care has been taken in its preparation. Although at the time of publication all routes followed public rights of way or permitted paths, diversion orders can be made and permissions withdrawn.

We cannot, of course, be held responsible for such diversion orders and any inaccuracies in the text which result from these or any other changes to the routes nor any damage which might result from walkers trespassing on private property. We are anxious though that all details covering the walks are kept up to date and would therefore welcome information from readers which would be relevant to future editions.

The simple sketch maps that accompany the walks in this book are based on notes made by the author whilst checking out the routes on the ground. They are designed to show you how to reach the start, to point out the main features of the overall circuit and they contain a progression of numbers that relate to the paragraphs of the text.

However, for the benefit of a proper map, we do recommend that you purchase the relevant Ordnance Survey sheet covering your walk. The Ordnance Survey maps are widely available, especially through booksellers and local newsagents.

INTRODUCTION

History is all around when you walk in Warwickshire, whether over its beautiful landscape of forests, fields and waterways or along the streets of its ancient towns and villages. This is the heart of England, and events over thousands of years have helped to shape it as it is today. Walking here is always a delight, but the notes that accompany the sixteen walks in this book will also explain much that might otherwise be missed and there are routes here to appeal to everyone.

In chronological order, the walks take you from the Stone Age mystery of the atmospheric Rollright Stones at Long Compton, to a stroll along the Grand Union Canal by the incredible 21 locks of the Hatton Flight which is not only a wonderful waterside walk but also an awe-inspiring insight into man's ingenuity. Romantic Kenilworth cannot be separated from the story of the love affair of Robert Dudley and Queen Elizabeth I, or Stratford upon Avon from Warwickshire's, and England's, greatest poet and playwright, William Shakespeare.

Each route has been chosen because it highlights a particular moment in Warwickshire's eventful past. All are circular and a grid reference is given for each starting point. Sketch maps indicate the route, though for more detail it is strongly advised that you carry the relevant Ordnance Survey map. Convenient places to park (usually free) have also been given, but if you have to park along the roadside, please do so with consideration for residents and other road users.

I have indicated where refreshments can be obtained on each walk, but it is advisable to carry a snack, and more importantly something to drink, especially on the longer routes. Remember also that, after rain or bad weather, country paths may be muddy or slippery so it is sensible to wear stout shoes.

I hope you will enjoy these walks into history and gain as much pleasure from them as I have had in devising them. Happy walking!

John Wilks

WALK 1

THE ROLLRIGHT STONES: A SACRED SITE IN THE STONE AGE

Length: 3½ miles

The Whispering Knights, the doorway to a Stone Age burial chamber

HOW TO GET THERE: The walk starts from the Red Lion public house in Long Compton, which is on the A3400, midway between Oxford and Stratford. The Red Lion is on the main road through the village.

PARKING: There is ample roadside parking on side roads in the village, but please park with consideration for residents.

MAP: OS Landranger 151 (GR 289324).

INTRODUCTION

This short but vigorous walk starts in the village of Long Compton before ascending to the ridge beyond. Passing the hamlet of Little Compton it arrives at the Rollright Stones, before returning to Long Compton. There are splendid views down over the plain. The walk is mainly on field paths, with two short sections of quiet lane, and there are two ascents and descents, one long and one short. Paths can be overgrown in summer.

HISTORICAL BACKGROUND

Although each Stone Age family had its own territory, they regularly met with other groups, sometimes for trade and sometimes for religious ceremonies. These meetings took place in massive open air enclosures, surrounded by an earthen bank or a ring of stones. One such site is the complex known as the Rollright Stones.

By 3000 BC, the late Stone Age, man had largely ceased to be a nomadic 'hunter-gatherer' and had evolved a more settled existence. He planted and harvested crops, especially cereals, rather than relying upon finding them in the wild, and bred animals for food. Woodland was cleared, to provide arable land and also to create openings where sweet new shoots would grow and attract wild game that could be easily hunted. People now lived in permanent timber homes. The population was still very small, with no more than 20,000 human beings in the whole of the British Isles. The well-drained gravels of the Upper Thames valley supported a comparatively large and prosperous population in the late Stone Age, but it was still widely scattered. They lived in family groups, each working their own land and isolated from their neighbours.

The site of the Rollright Stones consists of two main elements, a stone circle and an associated outlying stone. Nearby is a group of three stones that are the remains of an earlier burial mound. The circle was built on a high ridge above the forest, on the watershed between two highly populated valley systems. It was created by the cooperative labour of many communities working together, to serve the population of the whole locality rather than any single family or group.

A local legend has grown up around these stones: a king, marching over the Cotswolds with his army, met a witch, who told him that if he took seven strides to the north and could see Long Compton, he would be King of all England. Some of his men were unhappy at the offer, but the king strode off as bid. At the seventh stride he found his view blocked by an unseen fold in the land. The witch gleefully turned all of them into stone – the king, his loyal men standing in a circle nearby, and his uneasy knights, huddled whispering a little way off. Today's names for the stones are taken from this legend.

THE WALK

❶ With your back to the Red Lion, turn left along the road for 100 yards. At a 'school' road sign, turn left at a waymark post through a wooden gate, immediately to the right of the gateway to Daddys Bank. Follow the drive for 50 yards to go through a second gate. Keep ahead along the gravel track for 20 yards, until the track turns left, and then keep ahead up the field to a gate

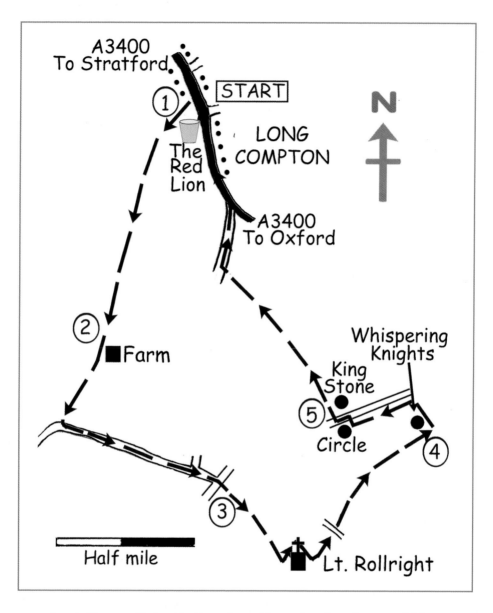

seen ahead. Cross a stile beside the gate and keep ahead up the next field, to cross a stile in the hedge ahead. Turn left for 10 yards, and then turn right up a track.

Behind and to the left of the farm visible on the skyline are the Rollright Stones. Even though there were fewer trees and less undergrowth in the Stone Age, the stone circle would still have been hidden from the valley below by the ridge line. However, it seems likely that some sort of ceremonial avenue would have been laid out on the ground, ascending to the ridge line and emerging at a single standing stone (now known as the King Stone) which marked the entrance to the site. Any such avenue has long since disappeared.

In 200 yards, where the track turns right to a gate, keep ahead up a clear footpath. Follow the footpath to a stile at the top of the field. Cross the stile and keep ahead up the slope. At a waymark post in 150 yards, bear half left, initially up the slope, then bear left beneath a hedge to reach a waymark post at a pedestrian gate.

2 Keep ahead towards a farm in front. Follow the path through a gate and keep ahead, the hedge close on your right and barns to your left. Beyond the barns enter a field and in 10 yards, at a waymark post, go half left across the field, aiming at the right-hand end of a line of trees seen opposite. Follow the path to cross a stile and reach the corner of a lane. Turn left and follow the lane for ½ mile, fine views opening up to your left. Pass a side lane to Long Compton on your left and continue ahead for 100 yards to reach a road. Cross the road to a stile beside a field gate and keep ahead down a grassy track.

3 Pass a barn on the left. Immediately afterwards ignore a track going off to the right but keep ahead downhill. At the bottom of the slope turn left in front of the church.

The tiny church of St Philip is Norman in origin, with the first recorded vicar assuming office in 1224. The manor of Little Rollright, together with this church, was originally the property of the Abbey of Evesham but after the Dissolution of the Monasteries the manor passed to the Dixon family. Inside the church are impressive monuments to John Dixon and also to Edward Dixon, the latter surrounded by his two wives and ten children.

Follow the track around the church. Where the track curves right, turn left up an enclosed footpath. Follow the footpath through two kissing gates and uphill to reach a lane. Cross the lane and go though the field gate opposite. Continue up the footpath. Follow the footpath up the slope and across a field. Pass through a line of trees and keep ahead across the next field.

4 At the end of the field, do not cross the stile ahead. Instead, turn left along a permissive path up the side of the field, the hedge close on your right, to reach the Whispering Knights.

The Whispering Knights are the remains of a burial chamber of the type known as a 'portal dolmen'. This was a communal burial mound, consisting of a small rectangular stone chamber, buried beneath a mound of earth, with the entrance marked by two huge upright stones, capped by a sloping roofstone, which projected beyond the uprights to form a porch. As the mound subsided over the centuries, the roofstone collapsed to give the shape seen today. Further stones, lining the sides of the burial chamber, have long since been removed.

The burial mound was built around 3000 BC, thus pre-dating the nearby stone circle. By this time families had settled down to practise farming in a specific area. They were few in number, and probably lived in a social grouping based around the extended family, which included the spirits of the dead as well as living members. The tomb would have been opened and closed many times, as successive generations were interred. It was traditional to put burial mounds upon high airy places, possibly for religious purposes but also perhaps to give the mounds an additional use as a territorial marker: the visible presence of the tomb announced the long-term inter-connection between a family unit and a specific area of land.

Continue along the path, the hedge still on your right, to reach a lane. Do not go onto the lane but turn left along a permissive path, the hedge and lane beyond on your right, to reach the King's Men.

The stone circle known as the King's Men was erected around 2200-2000 BC. It originally consisted of 22 tall monoliths, arranged in a 38-yard diameter circle. Centuries of weathering eroded the soft stones, many of which crumbled. Others were removed over the years by local farmers for building. In 1886 a well-meaning attempt was made to restore the circle, returning some looted stones and placing them in convenient gaps, and re-erecting fallen fragments to stand as new monoliths beside their original bases. Consequently, the circle as seen today looks little as it did when built. The main entrance to the circle opened to the north (towards the entrance kiosk), with a lesser entrance on the opposite, southern, side of the circle. In Neolithic times the valley to the south would have been lightly forested, with scattered circular huts standing amidst farmed clearings. A similar view would have greeted anyone looking off the ridge towards the north.

The Rollright Stones were a sacred site to Stone Age man, to whom 'religious' activity was a part of everyday life. All places were imbued with spirit, and most everyday activities had a ceremonial aspect. The spirits of the dead remained in the world, and played an active role in guiding the living. Some places, however, had particular religious significance, and monuments were built there for ceremonial purposes. This circle was one such sacred site, where religious ceremonies would have taken place. Many were concerned with marking the natural transformation of the seasons, which were to be celebrated and feared, but there were also many 'rites of passage' celebrated within the circle, rites connected with childbirth, puberty and marriage as well as death. The circle was there so that the community could celebrate the milestones of its individual members' lives, in the presence of their ancestors. The stones acted as a mystical wall, to contain the magic of the occasion whilst excluding everyday life. These ceremonies had the additional result of bringing together scattered families on a regular basis, where news and goods could be traded, marriages arranged, and tribal identity reinforced.

The stones are looked after by the Rollwright Stones Trust, and a small entry fee is requested.

From the stone circle turn right out to the lane. Cross the lane and go through a kissing gate to see the King Stone.

Several theories have been advanced to explain this twisted, 8 ft high, single standing stone: that it was part of a nearby chambered tomb, that it was the marker stone for a Bronze Age cemetery, that it was an astronomical marker stone associated with the stone circle. However, a careful look at the topography of the ridge you are standing on offers the most likely explanation.

The Rollright Stone circle was built here upon a high ridge to serve the ceremonial needs of communities living in the valleys on both sides. From the south, the circle would have been clearly visible for miles. But from the north, to anyone ascending the slope from the direction of modern Long Compton, the circle is hidden behind the crest of the ridge. The King Stone, however, is clearly visible on the skyline and once anyone has climbed from the valley bottom to the stone, the main northern entrance to the circle is in a straight line 80 yards in front.

⑤ Return to the lane. Turn right, the stone circle in the field on your left. Opposite the end of the layby, cross the road and go through a waymarked kissing gate onto a permissive Defra path. Keep ahead down the field, the hedge on your left. Look back and the function of the King Stone as a marker on the skyline can clearly be seen.

Go through a gate in the field corner and keep ahead down the next field. At the bottom of the field go through a gate and go half left down the next field, cutting the corner and eventually converging with the hedge on your left. Pass through a gate in the bottom corner. Continue down the next field to reach a metal field gate seen on the opposite side. Go through the gate and keep ahead to reach the end of a drive by dilapidated buildings. Keep ahead down the drive to reach another drive, and turn right. Follow the drive out to a lane and turn right. Follow the lane for ¼ mile to reach the main road. Turn left for 200 yards to return to the Red Lion.

WALK 2
WOOTTON WAWEN: CHRISTIANITY AND PAGANISM IN THE DARK AGES

Length: 4 miles

The church at Wootton Wawen dates from Saxon times

HOW TO GET THERE: Wootton Wawen is on the A3400, 1 mile south of Henley-in-Arden and 7 miles north of Stratford.

PARKING: There is roadside parking in front of the shop opposite the church, or in the village itself, although this is limited and consideration should be shown to residents.

MAP: OS Landranger 151 (GR 154633).

INTRODUCTION

From the village of Wootton Wawen, the walk crosses meadows and fields before entering Ansty Wood, with its spectacular displays of bluebells in season. After passing through the woods, the walk returns along a canal towpath to Wootton Wawen, with its fine manor house and splendid Saxon church. The walk is flat, and route-finding is easy.

HISTORICAL BACKGROUND

A hallowed burial ground in the Bronze Age, a sacred river and wood in the Iron Age, a Christian church from the days of the Saxons onwards – Wootton Wawen has been a religious centre since early man first settled in Warwickshire.

Although the exact nature of the religious beliefs of Bronze Age man is unknown, two aspects have been deduced with reasonable certainty: that there was a strong spiritual attachment to the land the people lived on, and that the dead were believed to have an ongoing presence within the living community. Important members of the tribe were interred within burial mounds called tumuli, and one such tumulus has been discovered in Wootton Wawen.

By the Iron Age, burial practices had changed, but veneration of the land continued. Deities were to be found in forests and groves, in marshes and lakes, rivers and springs. Druids, religious leaders of great power, conducted ceremonies in woodland groves. When the Romans conquered Britain they attempted to stamp out this form of nature worship but, although driven underground, it still

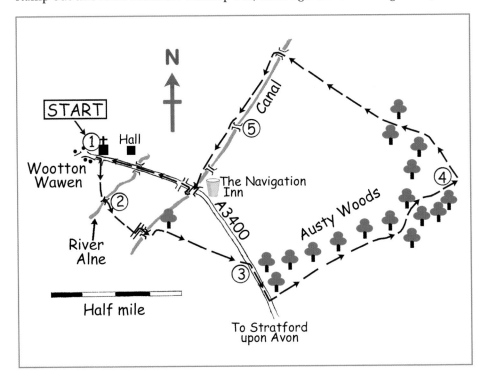

held great sway over the minds of the ordinary people living in the countryside. When Saxon settlers arrived in the 6th century they revived the old beliefs and incorporated them into their own pagan religion. Certain natural features, especially streams and woods, resumed their importance as holy sites. The village of Wotton Wawen was in the middle of one such holy site: Austy Wood.

When Christian missionaries were sent to Britain at the end of the 6th century, they often chose to capitalize upon the holiness of certain locations by building churches upon them. Crosses at which prayer meetings were held were erected on the boundaries of Austy Wood, and a church built next to the Bronze Age tumulus. The religion may have changed, but the importance of Wootton Wawen as a centre for worship continued unabated.

THE WALK

❶ Walk along the main road to the entrance to the church. With your back to the gates, cross directly over the road and go along the lane opposite, marked as a No Through Road and with a pillar box on the corner. In 20 yards go through a gate and keep ahead past the front of houses, to a kissing gate beside a field gate immediately in front of you. Keep ahead, a line of trees on your right hand, to another kissing gate, standing in splendid isolation in the middle of the path. Continue ahead along the embankment.

This embankment is part of a larger complex of banks and ditches built in the Iron Age above the ford across the river Alne. Their purpose is uncertain, but they may have been part of an Iron Age farm community. In the Middle Ages these embankments were given the name of Puck's Dyke, after the mythical pagan woodland spirit. Although the embankments themselves are unlikely to have had any religious significance, this medieval nickname signifies that Wootton Wawen was a holy place in pre-Christian times.

Follow the embankment to the river Alne and cross a footbridge.

The ancient Britons who first settled this area named the river 'Alwen', which translated as 'white', or 'bright', or 'shining', or a subtle combination of all three. The name reflected the sacred nature of the river. The present name, Alne, is a corruption of Alwen.

❷ On the far side of the bridge, go half right across the meadow to a kissing gate in the fence opposite. Go through the kissing gate and maintain your line of advance to a gate on the far side of the field. Go through a kissing gate beside the field gate. Keep ahead, a fence on your left hand, to another kissing gate in the corner of the field ahead. Continue along the next field, a fence on your left hand, to exit via a metal field gate onto a lane. Turn left along the lane for 50 yards and then turn right up an unmade drive, signed 'Private road no access to vehicles'. Cross the canal. Go through a gate and immediately turn left, to pass through a second gate in 10 yards. Keep ahead for 20 yards and then turn right in front of trees. Walk ahead, and where the trees end, go half right up the field to a stile visible on the skyline. Cross the stile and keep ahead across the next field towards a field gate in the fence opposite. Pass through the gate and go a quarter left, to a gate leading onto a road.

❸ Turn right along the road for 300 yards. Where the wood on the left ends, cross the road and go over a stile beside a gate. Keep ahead, passing between mature trees on your left and a new plantation on your right, to reach open scrubland. Keep ahead across the scrubland for ½ mile, gradually converging with the wood on your left. After ¼ mile ignore a wide drive into the woods, marked with a white sign, but keep ahead, now with the wood close on your left hand.

Today's wood is comparatively small, but when the village was founded in Saxon times, Wootton Wawen was largely surrounded by woodland, itself part of the huge Forest of Arden. The curious name of the village is derived from the fact that it was a settlement ('ton') in the woods and was part of the manor of a Saxon lord, Wagen or Wawen.

Where the boundary of the wood turns right across your path, keep ahead along a signed footpath into trees. Ascend the footpath through the trees, soon climbing quite steeply.

This area is today called Austy Wood but was originally called 'Horstow', meaning 'hallowed place', and indicates the likelihood that in pre-Christian times religious ceremonies were conducted within its woodland groves. Horstow Wood was a holy site for nature worshippers for a thousand years. The first Christian missionaries, sent to convert the pagan, tried to capitalise upon the holiness of the area. Preaching crosses were erected on the wood's boundaries, so that Christian services could be held in an area already associated with religious worship, and nearby Wootton Wawen became the obvious site to build a Christian church from which to spread the gospel.

Follow the path as it winds around the hillside, finally climbing to a T-junction of paths. Turn right and follow the path to a second T-junction, this one with footpath signs. Turn right for 20 yards, towards a gate into a field. Do not go through the gate, but instead turn left along a path, keeping just inside the edge of the woods.

❹ Follow the path as it turns left and descends, still just inside the woods, open fields to the right. Ignore side turns and follow the path, eventually to join a broader bridleway at a T-junction. Turn right along the bridleway. Follow the path as it leaves the woods and continues, tree-lined, between fields for ½ mile to reach the canal.

This path is the remains of a 'green lane', a medieval trackway running from Wootton Wawen to the outlying fields. Boundary hedges, now tree-lined, separated the track from the fields, and many centuries of use have eroded the trackway until it is lower than the fields it passes between.

Cross the canal bridge .Turn left and walk along the towpath, with the canal on your left.

⑤ In ¼ mile, pass bridge 52 and continue along the towpath.

Bridge 52 is of a design often still seen along the Stratford on Avon Canal, but rare elsewhere nowadays. Originally there was a 3-inch gap in the middle of the bridge: although it is now tarmacked over on the carriageway, the gap can still be seen in the handrails. Barges were initially drawn by a horse walking along the towpath; unlike on other canals, here no provision was made for the towpath to go under bridges, but instead the horse would walk around the top of the bridge. The tow rope was passed through the gap in the bridge, thereby avoiding unfortunate accidents.

In a further 300 yards, pass bridge 53 and continue along the canal, passing moorings for pleasure boats.

By the end of the 19th century the canal had fallen into disuse and was closed to commercial traffic. After the Second World War, the possibilities of canals for leisure purposes were recognized, and many sections of canal were cleared and reopened, in the process destroying the habitat of a wide range of wildlife that had colonized them.

Cross the viaduct, which carries the canal across the A3400.

Canals are surprisingly shallow. They rarely exceed a depth of 55 inches, and here as it crosses the viaduct the canal is only 40 inches deep.

At the end of the viaduct, turn sharp right and descend a steep path to reach the road opposite the Navigation Inn. Cross the road to the pavement opposite and turn left, passing under the viaduct. In 100 yards cross over the end of a lane. The Yew Tree farm shop and coffee shop is immediately on your right. Continue along the main road for 300 yards, to cross a bridge over the river Alne.

From the bridge, on your right you can see Wootton Hall and its surrounding park. The manor of Wootton was given to the powerful earls of Stafford after the Norman Conquest, although rarely visited by them and certainly never used as more than a summer retreat. With the family's disgrace in the reign of Henry VIII, the manor passed to the Harewell family, local gentry and civil servants, and then by marriage to the Smith-Caringtons, who built a new family home on the site of the present Hall. The Smith-Caringtons were staunchly Roman Catholic, and continued to practise the old religion in the face of the increasingly hostile Protestantism of Elizabeth's later reign. The Smiths were, however, pragmatists, and avoided involvement in the Gunpowder Plot of 1605, whose failure destroyed their Catholic neighbours, the Throckmortons of Coughton (see walk 12). Staunch Royalists in the Civil War, the family were temporarily disgraced during the Commonwealth, but with the restoration of Charles II the family fortunes soared. The present Hall was built in 1687 by the 2nd Lord Carington in the Palladian style popular at the time, and surrounded by a landscaped park, with the river Alne being diverted to create the ornamental pools and cascades seen today.

Unswerving support for the Stuarts led the then Lord Carrington into exile with James II in 1688, and continued support for the Jacobite cause eventually bankrupted the family. After the death of the last male Carington, the Hall passed through a number of owners, before being inherited in 1781 by Maria Smythe, later Mrs Fitzherbert, who became the morganatic wife of George, Prince of Wales, later George IV. In the 19th century the Hall was owned by a succession of Birmingham businessmen.

Continue along the road for a further 350 yards to reach the entrance to St Peter's church on your right.

The first church in Wootton Wawen was built between AD 723 and 736 as a minster or mission station, staffed by monks charged with bringing Christianity back to the county. The church of St Mary was built next to a prehistoric tumulus, a holy spot in the pre-Christian era, and was given 2,000 acres of surrounding farmland to support its activities. The first church was of timber and thatch, soon replaced by a stone structure, constructed from local red sandstone, which forms the basis of the church we see today.

After the Norman Conquest, Robert De Tosny was made Earl of Stafford and given Wootton. His family had founded the Benedictine monastery of Conches in Normandy, who in turn were given the minster of St Mary (this is a typical example of the Norman policy of using secular and spiritual powers in combination to overawe and subdue the conquered English population). The church was re-dedicated to St Peter-in-Chains, and a small priory built next to it to house an increased staff of monks. The church itself was greatly extended, with a huge chancel built to provide a chapel for the priory.

After about 1130, Wootton priory was reduced to only two monks, although they were helped by several lay brothers in their task of administering large secular estates.

The priory was always seen as an alien presence and suffered heavy penalties during the Hundred Years War. In 1443 the priory was finally closed down, and its assets, including the church of St Peter, given to Kings College, Cambridge. Now vicars were no longer French priests but learned Cambridge graduates, who became

embroiled in the religious upheavals of the following century. With one third of the congregation Catholics, supported by a Catholic lord of the manor, Elizabethan vicars to St Peter's often faced a daunting task in spreading the Protestant faith.

The present church is one of the finest Saxon churches left in the county. It has at its core a beautiful tower, Saxon at its base and topped in the Perpendicular style, and the interior reflects many centuries and styles. There are the remains of a medieval wall painting, a 14th-century font and a 15th-century pulpit.

After viewing the church, return to the main road and turn right back to the start.

WALK 3

BRINKLOW CASTLE AND THE NORMAN CONQUEST 1066

Length: 6 miles

The church of St John the Baptist, Brinklow

HOW TO GET THERE: The walk starts from the church in Brinklow, which is at the merging of the B4455 and the B4027, 4 miles east of Coventry.

PARKING: There is ample roadside parking on the main street.

MAP: OS Landranger 140 (GR 437796).

INTRODUCTION

From the village of Brinklow, with its 13th-century church and the remains of a splendid castle, this walk follows the canal to the village of Easenhall before returning across fields and past the ancient Newbold Revel estate. The walk is flat and route-finding simple.

HISTORICAL BACKGROUND

The paramount need for the new Norman monarchy in 1066 was to control England and nip any thoughts of revolt in the bud. Brinklow Castle was built as a result of this need.

William the Conqueror arrived in England with an army of only 6,000, many of them mercenaries who were soon dismissed. The conquest was not followed by a mass influx of settlers into the country, but was essentially the exchange of one aristocracy for another. The task confronting the Norman conquerors was a huge one, faced with subjugating a country with a large population and difficult communications with only a small number of men. The solution was to overawe the Saxons of England with their technical prowess. The Normans reintroduced into England the art of building in stone on a grand scale, lost after the Romans departed. Castles, town walls and churches sprang up across the country, buildings of a size and solidity largely unknown to the locals and designed to so impress them with the might of Norman civilization that rebellion would seem pointless.

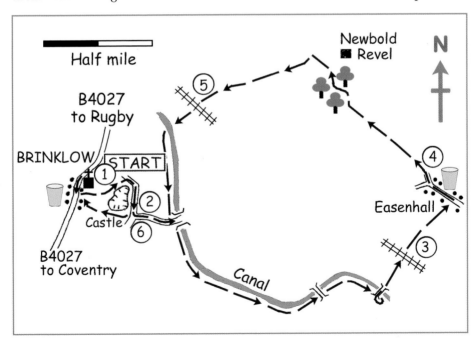

King William had won a personal kingdom for himself. He held it by rewarding his followers with lands captured from the defeated Saxons. These Norman landowners now had a vested interest in defending their new estates. His nobles were tasked with controlling the countryside and allowed a free hand to build private castles to defend their lands and sites of especial strategic importance. Robert de Mowbray was one of the small band of Norman nobles who had thrown in his lot with William and joined him in his venture to seize England. De Mowbray was well rewarded with the earldom of Leicester and extensive lands throughout the Midlands. His task was now to hold onto those lands, for himself and for his king. The Midlands of the 11th century were not the tame countryside we know today. Rich agricultural land was interspersed by areas of thick woodland and wild heaths. The mighty Forest of Arden covered much of the north and west of the area. Towns and villages were widely scattered, and communications between them, along narrow, rutted and often impassable lanes and trails, was difficult. The only real roads were those that had survived since Roman times, and the major one of these was the Fosse Way. Although only a shadow of its former glory, the Fosse was still the main artery through the Midlands, and control of this strategic road was vital. It was for this purpose that the mighty castle was built at Brinklow.

THE WALK

❶ Start at the church of St John the Baptist.

The first church in Brinklow was a subsidiary of the Saxon Kenilworth Abbey. After 1066 the Church followed the Norman army into England, and set about building and rebuilding churches, monasteries and huge cathedrals. Norman ecclesiastical architecture was on a far grander scale than anything achieved by the Saxons, and whilst church building was partly the result of genuine devotion, it was also part of the Norman policy of overawing the conquered population. The Saxon church of St John the Baptist in Brinklow was altered and enlarged in the decades following the Conquest, and then almost entirely rebuilt in the 13th century.

With your back to the church, turn left along the main road.

The village of Brinklow grew up on the old Roman road, the Fosse Way, one of the major Roman roads in Britain, which ran from the Wash to the Bristol Channel, bisecting the Midlands. The largely straight Fosse Way did a dogleg around an ancient British burial mound at Brinklow, on top of which the Romans built a signal station. The road fell into disrepair once the Romans abandoned Britain, but such was the genius of Roman civil engineering that it remained one of the few roads that could be used for most of the year. The Fosse Way was of paramount strategic importance to the Normans, and they built a castle on top of the old burial mound, on the site of the previous signal station.

Immediately before the Raven pub, turn left up an alley, 'Town Yard'. Follow the footpath to cross a stile and keep ahead up steps.

You are now crossing the outer ditch and rampart of Brinklow Castle. Most Norman castles were built on a 'motte and bailey' design. An earthen mound or 'motte' was created or a natural hill raised, on top of which a fortified keep was built. Around the keep was an open area, or 'bailey', surrounded by a line of fortifications. The bailey of Brinklow Castle was surrounded by a high earthen rampart, topped by a strong wooden palisade, with a ditch, 40 ft wide and 20 ft deep, around the outside as further protection. It is that ditch and rampart you are now crossing.

Go a few paces beyond the steps and pause where the view in front of you opens out.

You are looking across the Norman bailey, towards the motte, the mound ahead of you. The bailey of Brinklow Castle was two hectares in area, and unusually was divided into two areas or 'wards', with a ditch and rampart separating the two. The two wards would have contained numerous wooden buildings such as storerooms, workshops, stables, kitchens and barracks. You are now standing at the entrance to the outer ward.

Follow the footpath across an open space towards the mound ahead, passing through a second ditch and rampart.

This ditch and rampart separated the outer from the inner ward. When it was built the rampart was higher and steeper, and topped by a wooden palisade. The ditch was deeper, and crossed by a narrow and easily defended wooden bridge.

Continue forward to the earth-mound ahead.

This was the Norman motte, an artificial earthen mound on top of which a sturdy keep was built. The conical mound is 260 ft in diameter at its base, narrowing to 50 ft at its top, which is 60 ft high. Surrounding the motte was a deep ditch. The keep on top of the mound was a strong wooden structure, with a crenellated walkway from which archers could dominate both wards of the castle and which provided a vantage point across the surrounding countryside.

Robert de Mowbray, Earl of Leicester, had been given Brinklow immediately after the Conquest and by 1095 the castle was effectively complete. At the time it was the largest castle in the vicinity, and with its three lines of defences it must have been an awe-inspiring sight. Like the majority of Norman castles raised in the decades immediately after the Conquest, it was built quickly, with wooden walls and ramparts, which were usually replaced by stone as time permitted. There is no evidence that Brinklow's wooden fortifications were ever replaced, arguing that the mere existence of the castle was deterrent enough and that the Norman hold on the countryside hereabouts was never contested. Certainly, by 1173 Brinklow Castle was abandoned and allowed to decay.

Turn left and follow the waymark posts around the side of the mound. Turn left over a footbridge, and cross a stile into a lane. Turn right and follow the lane to a T-junction, where turn left.

② Follow the road for 350 yards to reach a bridge. Do not cross the bridge, but instead go down steps onto the canal towpath. Turn right and follow the canal towpath for 1 mile, to pass under bridge 35. Continue along the towpath for another 600 yards, to reach bridge 37. Go under the bridge, then turn right up the bank to cross the bridge. Keep ahead along a footpath across a field.

③ Cross the railway line via a bridge and then maintain your direction across the next field. Go through a kissing gate and then go half right across a third field to a kissing gate on the far side. Go along an alley, through another kissing gate and onto a road. Cross the road and turn left along the pavement. Follow the road through the village of Easenhall, passing the Golden Lion on your right.

④ Where the main road bends left, keep ahead along a side road, signed 'Bridle road to Stretton under Fosse'. Keep ahead though the gates of 'The Courtyard'. At the end of the concrete drive keep ahead along a stony path, bearing left to go through a gate. Turn right and follow the fence for 40 yards to pass through another gate. Keep ahead up the field, the fence on your right. Once over the brow of the hill, Newbold Revel House comes into sight ahead.

The estates of Newbold Revel were given by William the Conqueror to the Earldom of Leicester, and were in turn given by the Earl to lesser lords to hold as his feudal tenants. In 1433 the estate was inherited by Sir Thomas Mallory, author of the epic poem Morte D'Arthur. *The old and much extended Norman manor house was demolished in 1716 and replaced by the present building, which in turn was later altered and refurbished as a training college.*

In the bottom corner of the field, go through a gate and keep ahead along the next field, a hedge on your right. At the end of the hedge, keep ahead to the trees in front. Maintain your direction, the trees close on your left. Follow the path into the woods and immediately turn left over two footbridges. On the far side of the bridges turn right and follow the path, trees close on your right. In 150 yards turn right at a waymark post and follow a track back into the woods.

At the end of the woods keep ahead along the track, a sports ground on your right. Where further progress is barred by a gate, continue on a footpath to the left of the track. Follow the footpath to a drive. Do not go out onto the drive but immediately turn left through a wicket gate. Go half right to a waymark on a tree stump ahead, and then continue, trees soon on your left, following the path as it meanders along the left edge of a large field.

5 After ½ mile, follow the track as it passes under the railway, then keep ahead along a path to enter another field. Keep ahead, a hedge and stream on your left. Follow the path over a footbridge, the stream still on your left, and keep ahead to go through a culvert on a narrow walkway above the stream. On the far side of the culvert turn left up steps onto the canal bank and turn right. Follow the towpath across a bridge over a disused arm of the canal and keep ahead to reach bridge 34. On the far side of the bridge turn right up steps and then turn left along the lane. Retrace your outward steps to the T-junction with Ell Lane. Do not turn into the lane but keep ahead past the signpost to a waymark post on the opposite side.

6 Cross the stile and keep ahead across the field to a waymark post just visible on the far side.

The ridges and furrows in the field you are now crossing are the remains of strip lychetts. Medieval villages such as Brinklow were surrounded by two or sometimes three huge communal fields, which were divided into strips for ease of ploughing. Each villager would have owned one or more strips of land, scattered across each field to ensure that all villagers shared the good and the poor land. The length of each strip or 'furrow' was dictated in part by the lie of the land, but the breadth was always approximately 16½ ft, the width that a team of eight oxen could conveniently plough. Gradually over time the length became a standardised 'furrow length' or 'furlong'. Ownership of a team of oxen was beyond the means of most villagers, so resources were pooled at ploughing time. As the ox plough moved along the furrow, it threw up the earth into a bank, and these banks gradually became the boundaries between neighbours. These earthen banks are contemporary with Brinklow Castle and have remained outside the village of Brinklow since the Norman Conquest.

Pass the waymark and maintain direction along the top of the next field, the hedge and line of trees on your right. In the top right corner of the field drop down to cross a stile. Immediately turn left over a second stile and follow the footpath back to the main street in Brinklow.

WALK 4

TEMPLE BALSALL AND THE KNIGHTS TEMPLAR

Length: 7 miles

The Old Hall at Temple Balsall

HOW TO GET THERE: Knowle is on the main A4141 Birmingham to Warwick road, 2 miles south of Solihull. The walk starts from the church, on the main road.

PARKING: There is ample roadside parking in Knowle.

MAP: OS Landranger 139 (GR 183768).

INTRODUCTION

This pleasant walk starts in the charming old town of Knowle, and follows quiet country lanes and field paths to visit the Templar sites at Temple Balsall. It returns along the Grand Union Canal. There are no hills and route-finding is easy.

HISTORICAL BACKGROUND

There were many religious orders in the Middle Ages, but few are as romantic and as enigmatic in the public's mind as the Knights Templar, who gave their name to Temple Balsall.

A millennium ago a popular way for devout (and rich) Christians to give a solid example of their faith was to go on a pilgrimage to Jerusalem, a long and

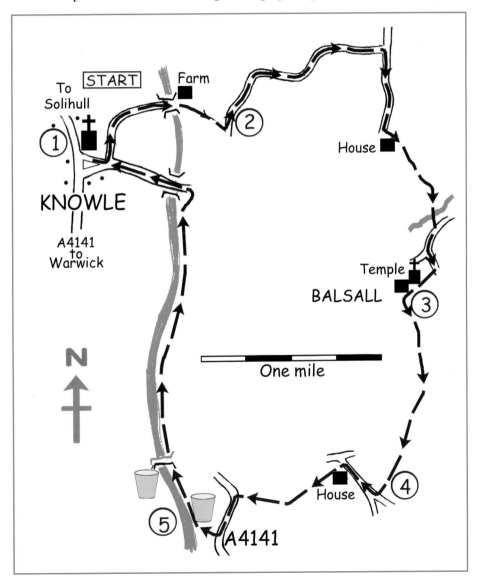

difficult journey fraught with danger, especially once they reached the Holy Land itself. Several military religious orders grew up to aid Christians travelling to Palestine. The Knights Templar were one such order, founded around 1118, when Hughes de Payen and eight other knights banded together to protect pilgrims. Their original headquarters were on top of the Temple mound in Jerusalem, hence 'Templars'.

In many ways the Knights Templar resembled a monastic order, with a programme of regular daily prayer and an obligation for charity and personal austerity, but they were also trained in the knightly skills, ready to fight if necessary to defend their faith. The Order soon gained the approval of the Pope and as the years passed they grew in numbers and wealth. When the loss of the 'Latin Kingdoms' (modern-day Palestine) forced the Order to relocate to the West, they established themselves as bankers to the various monarchs. Their independence and wealth made them arrogant and they eventually became hated by both clergy and secular authorities. In 1307 Philip IV of France accused the Order of heresy, thereby having an excuse to seize Templar land and property. Pope Clement V was bullied into issuing a papal edict dissolving the Order. The Templars continued to exist in England, Germany and Spain for some years after their expulsion from France, but they never regained their former influence and power, and, as the Holy Land ceased to be a major issue in European politics, the Order gradually withered. In England they survived, a remnant of their former glory, until the reign of Henry VIII, when they were swept away in the Dissolution of the Monasteries. All that remains today of the once-proud order are a few scattered buildings, and their name, given to places such as Temple Balsall.

THE WALK

❶ With your back to the church, turn left along the road (Kenilworth Road). Opposite the fuel station turn left into Kixley Lane. Follow this lane to cross the canal and reach Kixley Farm. Immediately before the gates to the farm, keep ahead down a grassy track to a kissing gate. Follow the footpath across the field and over a footbridge to a stile. Cross the stile and keep ahead up the next field, the hedge close on your right. At the end of the field cross a stile into a lane and turn left.

❷ Follow this quiet lane as it winds between fields and hedgerows. In ¾ mile, at a T-junction, turn right along Hob Lane. At North Lodge Piercil End, fork left along an unsurfaced track. Follow the track to a ford, crossing by a footbridge. Keep ahead along the track to a road. Turn right and follow the road around a right-hand bend, then turn left into Fen End Road East. Follow the road past a school and then immediately turn right onto a footpath, a drive on your left. Follow the footpath past the Knights Templar sites, but firstly, look to your right to see the Leveson Almshouses.

The Templars had owned the manor of Temple Balsall since the 12th century, building a church and a manor house, supported by the feudal dues of the local population. The estate was seized by Henry VIII as part of the general process known as the Dissolution of the Monasteries, and given to his last wife, Queen Catherine Parr. It then passed to Robert Dudley, Earl of Leicester and major local magnate, and in turn to his grand-daughters Lady Anne Holbourne and Lady Katherine Leveson. In her will Lady Katherine left instructions and funds for the erection of a hospice to house 20 widows or spinsters 'of goodly living', who were to be paid an annual pension of £8. Additionally, there was to be a school for 20 poor boys. School and hospice were under the control of a salaried minister.

The original hospice was built by 1679, but to such shoddy workmanship that it had to be almost entirely rebuilt in 1725. The architect on this latter occasion was Francis Smith, who had rebuilt St Mary's church, Warwick after the fire (see walk 6). Under Smith, the building was much enlarged and improved. Two additional wings were added in the late 18th century, providing additional facilities and accommodation for more staff. The Master's House, the last surviving part of the original building, was replaced in 1835. The splendid building we see today has nothing left of the Tudor original, but is still true to Lady Katherine's intentions, providing sheltered accommodation and, if required, nursing care for 40 elderly people.

Continue along the pathway to reach the church.

The church of St Mary the Virgin was built by the Templars as a private chapel, in which to carry out the programme of daily prayer that was an essential part of their order. The church was abandoned at the Dissolution, and made derelict when its lead roof was removed. It was restored by Lady Katherine Leveson to provide a place of worship for the residents of the hospice she was building next door. The minister of the church was also warden of the hospice. The church was heavily altered in the 19th century, and the church you see today is largely Victorian.

A few yards further along the path, pause and look at the old building on your right, next to the church.

This is the Old Hall, built by the Templars in the 12th century. It was originally a half-timbered building, erected to house the Knights who controlled this manor. Although a brick facing was put on the building in the 18th century, the original timber structure is still there. Today the Old Hall is used as offices and a community centre for the residents of the almshouses.

❸ Follow the footpath to a gate. Just before the gate, turn left through a kissing gate and follow the footpath, trees close on your left. Cross a stile beside a gate and maintain your direction, along a broad grassy path. At a telegraph pole, ignore the inviting track ahead of you and instead turn right along a grassy track. The track narrows to a footpath. Keep ahead, a hedge on your left. Follow the footpath to a stile leading into a lane.

❹ Turn right along the lane. In a few yards, bear right along the lane for another ¼ mile. Just before a road junction, turn left onto a gravel track to the right of the gates to Park Corner House. Follow the track, soon becoming enclosed and unsurfaced, downhill to join a broader track at a gate. Turn right along this second track, more open and better surfaced. Follow the track to the gates of a farm on your right, and keep ahead through a metal gate. Follow the enclosed grassy path out to a road. Cross over this busy main road and turn left along the pavement for 300 yards, and then turn right along the drive to the Blackboys public house. Keep ahead through the car park to reach the canal.

❺ Turn right along the towpath, passing the pub's beer garden. Follow the towpath under a bridge (with the Herons Nest pub on the opposite bank) and keep on to reach Knowle locks.

Birmingham was at the centre of the canal network that sprang up in the late 18th and early 19th centuries. Not only did the growing city require the import of raw materials and the export of finished goods, but it was also astride the main arteries of communication that connected the north of England with the Severn valley and with London. Unfortunately, Birmingham stands on a plateau, thus requiring a large number of locks to lift canal boats up and down. The Grand Union Canal runs from Birmingham to London, and has over 150 locks, 46 of them in Warwickshire alone. The most spectacular flight are a few miles down-canal, at Hatton (see walk 14), but the short, steep flight here at Knowle is also very impressive.

In 250 yards after the top lock, go up the track onto bridge 71. Turn left across the bridge and follow the road for ½ mile, ignoring side turns, to return to Knowle church.

WALK 5

BEAUDESERT CASTLE AND THE BARONS' REVOLT

Length: 5 miles

Beaudesert Castle's motte

HOW TO GET THERE: Henley-in-Arden is on the A3400, 8 miles north of Stratford.

PARKING: The walk starts from the free car park, clearly signed from the main road.

MAP: OS Landranger 151 (GR 151659).

INTRODUCTION

This walk starts in the lovely old market town of Henley-in-Arden, and climbs through the evocative remains of Beaudesert Castle. It then goes across fields and along an especially attractive stretch of canal towpath before returning to Henley. There is one short steep ascent right at the beginning of the walk, otherwise it is largely on the flat, on field paths, towpaths and quiet lanes. Route-finding is easy.

HISTORICAL BACKGROUND

On the outskirts of the market town of Henley-in-Arden stand the imposing remains of Beaudesert Castle, forever associated with England's greatest nobleman and leader of the Barons' Revolt, Simon de Montfort.

As his long reign continued, Henry III, unreliable, inconsistent and prone to outbursts of fury, became increasingly unpopular with his barons. The

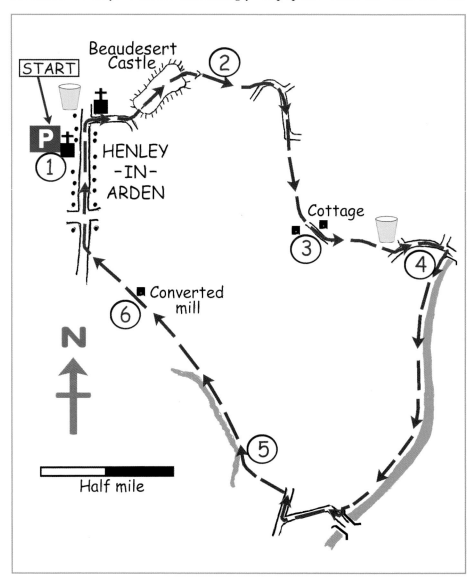

antagonism towards Henry was part of a much wider question, namely how much power should a king have to rule as he wished and how much say should the hereditary nobility have in the government of the land. Henry's father King John had been forced to give some powers to the nobles in the Magna Carta, and Henry was deeply opposed to making any further concessions. His increasingly high-handed and autocratic actions could not be accepted by a faction of the nobility, who found a leader in Henry's brother-in-law, Simon de Montfort, Earl of Leicester, foremost soldier in England, whose lands covered much of the Midlands. Political opposition shortly turned to armed revolt, and in 1264 the King was defeated at the Battle of Lewes. Henry and his heir, Prince Edward, were imprisoned, and Simon de Montfort became effectively ruler of England.

The following year Prince Edward escaped, fled to Worcester, and raised an army from amongst those barons who resented de Montfort's power. To meet this threat de Montfort slowly advanced from London, whilst his eldest son gathered forces in the Midlands. Levees were raised, and troops sent from allies, including Peter de Montfort, Simon's cousin and the Lord of Beaudesert. This second rebel army assembled at Kenilworth Castle, the mightiest of the de Montfort castles. However, Prince Edward moved with decisive speed, preventing the two baronial armies from joining by intercepting Simon de Montfort at Evesham. In the ensuing battle, de Montfort was killed and his army destroyed.

Prince Edward then returned north. Beaudesert and other outlying de Montfort strongholds were occupied and many of them partially destroyed, and the remaining rebel forces were trapped in Kenilworth Castle. After a six month siege the castle fell, and the baronial revolt was over.

THE WALK

❶ From the car park return to the main road. Cross at the traffic lights and turn left towards the church of St John the Baptist, then turn right into a No Through Road to the side of the church. Follow the road away from the High Street. Where the road bends right, ignore an enclosed footpath going ahead but instead go left through a kissing gate and climb the sleep slope ahead.

The slope you are climbing is the outer rampart of Beaudesert Castle. Beaudesert was originally a Norman motte and bailey castle, with an earthen mound or motte, on top of which was a fortified keep, surrounded by a walled enclosure, or bailey. However, Beaudesert differed from the standard motte and bailey in a number of ways. Firstly, it was built upon the end of a steep natural ridge, giving it initial height which was then further increased by the addition of the motte. Secondly, it was built in an hour-glass shape, with an elevated outer bailey, separated from the inner bailey and the still higher keep by a dry moat. You are climbing up the natural slope to the outer bailey. When first built, just after the Norman Conquest, the slope would have been steeper and cleared of vegetation, and topped by a strong wooden palisade. A dry moat was dug around the bottom of the slope, adding a further line of defence.

Pause at the top of the slope.

You are now at the southern end of the outer bailey (the flat plateau ahead of you). There is some evidence that this plateau was the site of an Iron Age hill fort, a natural defensive position eventually utilized by the invading Normans. The land was part of the feudal holdings given by William the Conqueror to his supporter Henry de Newburgh, Earl of Warwick, who in turn gave it to his vassal and nephew, Thurstan de Montfort. This site was a clear area in the middle of the vast Forest of Arden, and was named Beaudesert, or 'beautiful wasteland', by de Montfort.

Follow the clear path across the plateau, and down through a dip.

The slight dip is all that is left of the dry moat that separated the inner and outer baileys. Both baileys would have been surrounded by wooden palisades, and a retractable wooden bridge crossed the moat.

Follow the path as it rises to a higher point at the end of the ridge.

You are now on the artificial mound of the motte, on top of which was built the strong keep. Like the baileys, the keep was first built of wood, but in the middle of the 12th century Peter de Montfort, grandson of the castle's original builder, replaced the wooden walls of the keep with stone for added fortification. The bailey walls remained wooden.

Follow the path down steps and climb a second slope.

Beyond the keep mound, and separated from it by a dry moat originally 30 ft deep, is another mound, upon which was built a strong outer gatehouse, or barbican. This was the original entrance to the castle (we have come in through the back wall), and a drawbridge spanned the moat between the barbican and the keep.

Follow the path down the outer slope of the earthwork and up the slope opposite.

Pause at the bench at the top of the slope and look back, where the shape of Beaudesert Castle can quite clearly be seen. Peter de Montfort supported his cousin Simon against Henry III, and died in 1265 during the campaign which finally suppressed the Barons' Revolt. Beaudesert Castle was partially destroyed by royal forces in the aftermath of that revolt, and the lands seized, but Peter's son, also called Peter, swore allegiance to King Henry and soon had his estates restored to him. He rebuilt the castle, which remained in the de Montfort family for another century. In 1369 ownership reverted to its feudal overlord, the Earl of Warwick, and the castle went into decline. By the 1540s nothing remained of this once splendid fortification.

② Just past the bench, go right over a stile. Keep ahead along the field edge, the hedge close on your right. In the far corner of the field, cross a stile. Go half left across the next field to a stile leading into a lane. Turn left and follow the lane around a corner. Ignore a side turn to the left but keep ahead around a right bend. In 200 yards, where the lane bends sharp left, keep ahead through a pedestrian gate beside a wooden gate across a drive. Keep ahead along the drive and at a second gate in 100 yards, keep ahead through a pedestrian gate to its right. Follow the enclosed footpath past buildings. Keep ahead along a grassy track to cross a stile beside a barn. Keep ahead across the next field to go through a gate seen opposite. Then keep ahead along the next field, the hedge on your left, to reach a stile beside a metal field gate in the field corner.

③ Follow the gravel drive past houses and keep ahead along a tarmac lane. Immediately after passing the entrance drive to Hillside Cottage, with its double garage, turn left over a stile into trees. Follow the path through the trees into a field. Keep ahead down the long field, the tree-lined boundary close on your left. At the far end of the field cross a stile and go half right down the next field, towards a half-timbered building seen ahead. Go through a metal field gate to reach the road beside the Crabmill Country Restaurant. Turn left along the road, crossing a side road. In 200 yards, opposite a second lane on the left (No Through Road), cross the road and go through a field gate.

④ Turn right down onto the canal bank. Follow the towpath for 1½ miles to reach bridge 50. Turn right down a tarmac lane, passing a house on the left and following the lane around a left-hand bend. Follow the lane for another 400 yards to reach a road. Turn right along the road for 100 yards, and then turn left at a waymark post though a kissing gate. Go half right across the field, aiming for the right-hand corner of a line of trees seen ahead. Continue past the trees to reach a river bank and turn right.

⑤ Follow the river for nearly ½ mile, to finally enter a field at a waymark post. Turn right and then left with the field boundary. When the hedge on the right ends, keep ahead for 5 yards and then fork left on a path across the field, aiming for a white building seen on the far side. In the corner of the field, enter a drive and immediately turn left through a gate. Follow the tarmac drive past houses (a converted mill).

⑥ Where the drive turns left, turn right across a parking area to a bridge across the mill stream. Follow the enclosed footpath out to a sports field. Go half right across the field, aiming at the right-hand corner, where a kissing gate leading onto a road finally becomes visible. Turn right and follow the road to traffic lights. Cross at the lights and keep ahead along the High Street.

You are following the main street of Henley-in-Arden. The town's origin is found in its name – a 'hen' or hamlet in a 'ley' or forest clearing, in the middle of the vast Forest of Arden, which in the Middle Ages covered much of the Midlands. The settlement grew in importance with the building of Beaudesert Castle, and in 1140 it was given a charter to hold a weekly market. Although the town was burned in 1165 during Prince Edward's advance through the de Montfort lands to Kenilworth, it was quickly rebuilt, and continued to grow in size, until by the 16th century it was a flourishing market town. The 15th-century Guildhall in the High Street is a survivor of the town's past splendour, and the nearby church of St Nicholas is Norman in origin.

Follow the High Street, passing the Guildhall and St Nicholas' church on the left and then turning left back to the car park.

WALK 6
WARWICK THE IMPREGNABLE, AND ITS MEDIEVAL TOWN

Length: 3 miles

Warwick Castle seen from the route

HOW TO GET THERE: The walk starts from the car park on the south side of Warwick, off the Banbury Road A425.

PARKING: The pay and display car park in St Nicholas Park, Warwick, is signed throughout the town.

MAP: OS Landranger 151 (GR 288647).

INTRODUCTION

Historic streets, quiet alleys, and parkland enhance a walk within the borders of this green and leafy town. The route passes the major historical sites, naturally including the castle, and takes in Warwick's beautifully preserved architectural heritage. Walking and route-finding are simple.

HISTORICAL BACKGROUND

Warwick town was born out of strategic necessity. In AD 914 Queen Aethelflaeda of Mercia inherited the daunting task from her father Alfred the Great of defending the Anglo-Saxon kingdoms from the Danes. She decided to build ten burghs, fortified towns, at strategic points along her border, to act as military centres for the defence of Mercia. Warwick had few advantages as a settlement: it was not on a natural trade route, it was not on a Roman road (then the only highways in Anglo-Saxon England), and the river Avon was not navigable. But what it did have was the best defensive site for miles around – a high rocky bluff overlooking a weir that blocked the river – and it was on top of this bluff that Aethelflaeda built her burgh.

A ditch and rampart was built around the top of the hill, inside which a town grew up. A new shire was created on this borderland, with Warwick as its county town, with the right to hold markets and to mint currency. Warwick, laid out to a simple plan with four main streets meeting at a central crossroads, continued to grow and by the time of the Norman Conquest was a flourishing town with a population of 2,000. The Normans increased the town's defences, replacing the wood and earth ramparts with stone walls, and building a castle on the southern side of the town. Three strong gates penetrated the town walls, to north, east and west, whilst on the southern side of the town the castle grew ever bigger. By 1208 there was a bridge over the Avon, and housing was spreading along the roads leading downhill from the town gates.

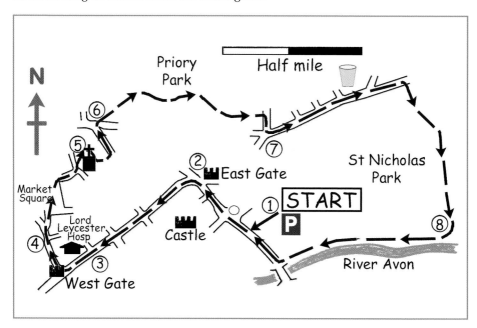

Warwick Castle was progressively enlarged, incorporating the latest developments in military architecture, until it became one of the greatest medieval fortresses in Britain. Meanwhile, Warwick itself grew in size and prosperity, but in 1694 it was devastated by a fire which swept through its tightly packed wooden buildings and destroyed much of the town. Such was the wealth and importance of Warwick, that over the next ten years it was largely rebuilt, with fine brick and stone buildings of the latest style replacing the old medieval timber ones. However, in the decades that followed, Warwick declined in importance. The Industrial Revolution largely passed it by, and by the 19th century it was becoming overshadowed by nearby Leamington. In consequence, it escaped wholesale redevelopment, and has retained many of its fine 18th-century buildings. Today, Warwick has some of the finest architecture of the William and Mary era in England, as well as the country's best preserved medieval castle.

THE WALK

❶ From the car park, return along the access drive to the main road. Cross at pedestrian lights and turn right to reach the castle entrance.

William the Conqueror recognised the strategic importance of Warwick and ordered the building of a castle adjoining the existing Saxon burgh. The castle remained the property of the Crown, and was controlled on the king's behalf by a constable, usually the Earl of Warwick. The original castle was a standard Norman motte and bailey, a keep on an artificial mound, surrounded by a walled courtyard, but over the next two centuries its size and defences were progressively increased. In 1265 the earldom of Warwick passed to Thomas Beaucamp, and he and his son, also called Thomas, were responsible for building most of the castle seen today. A magnificent new frontage was added on the eastern end, two huge towers – Guys Tower and Caesars Tower – were built as residences on the north side, with an enlarged gatehouse between the two, the surrounding curtain wall was greatly raised, and a new Great Hall built. By the time the castle passed to Richard Beaucamp, at the beginning of the 15th century, it was the most magnificent castle in England.

Richard Beaucamp, Earl of Warwick, was a close friend of Henry V who distinguished himself in the wars with France. On his death the castle and earldom passed to his son-in-law, Richard Neville, who as 'Warwick the Kingmaker' played an important part in putting Edward IV on the throne during the Wars of the Roses. Neville married two of his daughters to the two brothers of King Edward, and on his death the castle passed firstly to the elder brother, George, Duke of Clarence, and then to the younger brother Richard, Duke of Gloucester (later Richard III). Richard started but never completed the last major changes to the castle fortifications, a state-of-the-art fortress within a fortress.

After the accession of Henry VII there was no Earl of Warwick until 1547, when Henry VIII bestowed the title upon John Dudley. As Duke of Northumberland, Dudley later went on to become Lord Protector of England, the most powerful noble in England during the reign of Edward VI. Dudley was executed in 1553 for attempting to usurp Queen Mary and put his daughter-in-law, Jane Grey, on the throne, and his surviving sons were imprisoned for the rest of Mary's reign. With the accession of Elizabeth I, the family's fortunes were restored, and Dudley's eldest surviving son, Ambrose, became Earl of Warwick, and played a significant part in the history of the town. On Ambrose's death in 1589 the castle reverted to royal ownership.

In 1604 James I gave the castle (but not the earldom) to Sir Faulke Greville, later Lord Brooke. The castle was by now dilapidated, but at great expense Greville restored it to its former magnificence. Faulke's son Richard was a staunch Parliamentarian during the Civil War and the castle was a key Roundhead stronghold. After the end of the war, Warwick Castle ceased to have any strategic significance, but it remained the home of the Greville family until 1978.

Warwick Castle is open daily 10 am to 6 pm (5 pm in winter). There is an admission charge.

Before moving on, look left down Mill Street.

In the Middle Ages this old street ran alongside the town walls, curving down to the river beside the weir, where the town mill stood, and where the old town bridge crossed the river Avon. It escaped the fire and many of its buildings date from the 17th century. With its cobbled street and half-timbered houses, it gives a good impression of what Warwick once looked like.

Continue past the castle entrance uphill to traffic lights.

This is the site of the East Gate of the old Saxon burgh. When the Normans replaced the earthen Saxon walls with stone, they also built three strong gatehouses, to east, west and north. This, the eastern gate, was rebuilt in the 15th century upon the original Norman foundations, and a chapel, dedicated to St Peter, built on top of it. The chapel was itself rebuilt in 1788, at which time the gatehouse was drastically refaced and redesigned.

❷   Turn left along Jury Street.

This is the main east-west road that ran through Saxon and Norman Warwick. The fire of 1694 started at the western end of town, and, swept along by strong south-westerly winds, consumed much of the town. The half-timbered building that now houses Pizza Express is of pre-fire origin, and marks the place where the fire was finally halted. As you will notice as you walk along Jury Street, all the buildings to the west of Pizza Express are post-fire. Many of them date from the 1694–1704 reconstruction of the town, and are still fine examples of the so-called 'William and Mary' architectural style.

Follow Jury Street to crossroads, with the Tourist Information Office on the left.

This road junction was the old Saxon crossroads in the middle of Warwick. The east-west road still follows its original course through town. The straight course of the north road (to your right) has been interrupted by the building of the tower of St Mary's church, whilst the southern road was truncated in 1779, when Lord Brooke extended the castle grounds across it. Glance left down Castle Street. The half-timbered building you see is Oken House, built by a wealthy local businessman and benefactor, Thomas Oken. The oldest parts of the building are 14th-century and it is another survivor of the fire of 1694.

Cross the road at the zebra crossing and turn left. Continue along the main road to pass the Unitarian chapel on your left, built on the site where the 1694 fire started.

❸ Continue along the road to reach the half-timbered Lord Leycester Hospital.

The public life of many medieval towns was controlled by guilds, self-help organizations that looked after the spiritual and physical needs of their members and often of the town as a whole. Although Warwick had less control over its own affairs than many towns (the Earls of Warwick playing an active role in the town's governance), powers were little by little given over to Warwick's two guilds, the Guild of St George and the Guild of the Holy Trinity. By 1413 these had combined to form the United Guilds, and this magnificent set of buildings was erected to house them, with a Great Hall for guild meetings, a schoolroom and other public rooms. When the Guild was abolished during the Reformation, the Master of the Guild Thomas Oken transferred its property to the town council, thereby saving it from seizure.
  However, this salvation was only temporary. Robert Dudley, Earl of Leicester and owner of nearby Kenilworth Castle, had led an unsuccessful military campaign in the Netherlands and upon his return to England, conceived the idea of a hospice to accommodate ex-soldiers. The Warwick guildhall appealed to him as a suitable building, and was highhandedly given to him by his brother Ambrose, the Earl of Warwick. The guildhall was renamed the Lord Leycester Hospital (or 'hospice') and functioned as almshouses until 1956.

The Lord Leycester Hospital is open daily except Mondays and Bank Holidays, 10 am to 4 pm in winter, 10 am to 5 pm in summer. There is an admission charge.

Continue ahead through the arch under the West Gate.

This is the site of the western gate into the Saxon burgh, and like the East Gate, a western gatehouse was built by the Normans to defend the entry into the town. The arched passageway which carried the road under the gatehouse was channelled out of the limestone bluff on which Warwick was built, and the vaulting in its ceiling is 14th-century. In the 15th century the chapel of St James was built on top of the gatehouse, and became the chapel of the Guildhall, and later the Lord Leycester Hospital. Unlike the East Gate, the West Gate avoided 19th-century reconstruction, and, again unlike the East Gate, its chapel forms a pleasing architectural whole with the gatehouse itself. On the far side of the arch is West Street, the expansion westwards of Warwick which started in the 13th century and which contains a number of medieval half-timbered buildings.

On the far side of the arch turn right.

Behind the almshouses on your right, and joining onto the West Gate, the sole surviving section of the old town walls can be seen. As the strategic importance of Warwick declined, the walls were gradually dismantled to provide building material.

④ Follow the road up to the bus station. Fork half right, taking the road between Boots and Hydropool, to reach the town square.

Warwick was granted a licence to hold a twice-weekly market in Saxon times, and a market square was an integral part of the Saxon and Norman towns. There is still a market held here every Saturday. The building on your right as you enter the square, now the town museum, was built in 1670 as a market hall, to control the affairs of the market.

Go diagonally right across the square and leave by the top right corner, behind Lloyds No1 pub. Keep ahead to reach St Mary's church.

In 1123 there were nine churches in Warwick, of which the oldest and largest was St Mary's. In that year it became a collegiate church, with a college of canons under a dean. The original Saxon building had been extensively rebuilt by the Normans, and in the 14th century, by now the main church within Warwick's walls, it was further modified by the Beaucamp Earls of Warwick. The chancel and chapter house were rebuilt between 1381 and 1396, in an early example of the Perpendicular style of architecture. A chantry chapel, where monks could pray for the soul of the departed, was built to house the tomb of Richard Beaucamp, who died in 1439. This chapel was one of the few parts of the church to survive the fire of 1694, when the nave, aisles, transepts and tower of the church were destroyed. The church was rapidly rebuilt, but almost immediately the new tower developed cracks and had to be taken down. It was replaced by the present tower, which, in order to support its own weight, was built out into the road, thus interrupting the former straight run of road from the north gate to the crossroads. Today St Mary's is Warwick's parish church and is world famous for its Beauchamp chapel, one of the finest medieval chapels still in existence.

St Mary's is open to visitors. Its 174-ft tower can be climbed for a fee, and offers magnificent views across Warwick.

❺ Turn left in front of the church and in 10 yards turn right through a gate into the churchyard. Follow the path as it curves around the church. In the bottom corner keep ahead and then immediately turn left down a walled alley, a surviving example of the many that criss-crossed medieval Warwick. Follow the alley out to a road.

This road is called The Butts, and follows the course of a medieval open space, just inside the walls, where archery was practised. An edict of Edward I made regular practice with the longbow by able-bodied men compulsory, thereby creating a population of trained archers from which a fighting force could be assembled when required. This regular target practice, firing at straw targets or 'butts', enabled the English bowman to dominate the battlefields of Europe.

Cross the road and turn left along The Butts to reach a main road, the Punch Bowl on your right.

To your left is the site of the north gate of the town. Nothing now remains of it apart from the fine 17th-century building that bears its name, Northgate House.

❻ Cross the road to the front of the police station. Take the grassy path to the right of the station and its access drive, leading into Priory Park.

A small priory once stood on the northern side of Warwick, just outside the town walls. It was dissolved in 1537 as part of the general Dissolution of the Monasteries. With its glass and lead sold off, and its stones plundered for building, it rapidly disappeared, although its foundations have been excavated.

Bear right, a wall and house close on your right, to reach a gravel path. Turn right along the path, soon tarmac. Follow the path down to gates, and keep ahead along a drive to a road. Turn right along the road to traffic lights.

Opposite you is St John's House, today a museum. It was built in 1626 on the site of a medieval hospital.

❼ Turn left across the road to the Crown and Castle and then keep ahead along the road, the pub on your left.

This street is called Coton End, once a separate hamlet outside the walls of Warwick Town ('coton' is Anglo-Saxon for cottages, which formed a separate district or 'end'). The fire failed to reach this far, and many medieval half-timbered buildings can still be seen along this road.

Continue along the road to reach the 16th-century Millwright Arms, the oldest public house in Warwick. Cross the road at pedestrian lights and turn left. In 200 yards, at the next set of lights, turn right onto a footpath leading into a park. Follow the footpath across the park, crossing a cross track and continuing ahead to reach the river Avon at a footbridge.

❽ Do not cross the footbridge but instead turn right and follow the footpath along the river bank. Pass a café and boathouse on your left and climb steps ahead to the road. Cross the road and turn left for a few yards onto the bridge for the classic view of the castle.

The old medieval bridge over the Avon was constantly in need of repair. In 1779 Lord Brooke offered to build a new bridge, on which you are now standing, provided it was erected several hundred yards downstream, the main road similarly diverted, and he was allowed to extend the castle grounds into the space thus vacated. The remains of the old bridge can be seen in the river below the weir, and the medieval settlement of Bridge End, into which the old bridge led but which was effectively cut off when the new bridge replaced it, can be seen on the left bank.

With your back to the castle, turn left and follow the pavement to pedestrian lights. Cross the road and keep ahead back to the car park.

WALK 7
MAXSTOKE PRIORY AND THE DESTRUCTION OF THE MONASTERIES

Length: 8 miles

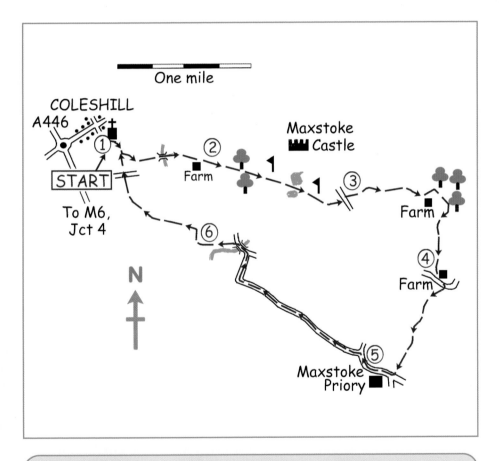

HOW TO GET THERE: The walk starts from Coleshill church. Coleshill is just east of the A446, 1 mile north of junction 4 of the M6.

PARKING: There are two free car parks in Coleshill.

MAP: OS Landranger 139 (GR 201891).

INTRODUCTION

Although quite long, this walk is easy underfoot and with simple route-finding. It starts in the town of Coleshill, and goes to the village of Maxstoke over field paths and farm tracks, passing near to Maxstoke Castle en route. In Maxstoke the remains of the priory can be seen, and then the walk proceeds along quiet country lanes and over fields back to Coleshill.

HISTORICAL BACKGROUND

During the Middle Ages the Church was the richest landowner in England after the King, all too often using its spiritual power to protect its secular interests and neglecting its pastoral duties. In the reign of Henry VIII an increasing need to reform the organization of the Church coincided with the King's political needs, with disastrous results for religious houses such as Maxstoke Priory.

Henry VIII was a devout Catholic, who had been awarded the title of 'Defender of the Faith' by the Pope for his erudite and vigorous defence of Catholicism against the doctrines of Luther. Moreover, despite abuses of power, many religious houses did perform important work helping the poor and needy. Henry had no inclination to join the attack on the Church known as the Reformation that was sweeping Northern Europe. However, dynastic considerations were to force his hand.

For most of the previous century, England had been racked by the civil war later known as the Wars of the Roses, as powerful factions vied to control the Crown. The reign of Henry's father, Henry VII, had seen several pretenders to the throne raising rebellion, and Henry VIII's own right to the throne had been contested. Henry was desperate for an heir whose claim to the throne would be undisputed, and this meant a son. Although there was no constitutional reason why a Queen should not rule England, it had never happened successfully, and it was doubted that a woman would be strong enough to rule. Many years of happy marriage had given Henry only one live child, his daughter Mary, and, with no prospect of a son, the spectre of his dynasty being challenged after his death drove Henry to desperate measures. In 1527 he decided to divorce his beloved wife, Queen Catherine of Aragon, and marry the younger Anne Boleyn, who held out the prospect of producing a male child.

Unfortunately for the King, the Pope rejected Henry's ingenious arguments as to why his marriage to Catherine was illegal and refused to grant a divorce. To influence the Pope, Henry started to put pressure on the Church in England, increasingly curbing its powers and attacking its privileges. For five years the Pope resisted his steadily increasing campaign against the Church, until in 1533 he finally excommunicated Henry. The King responded by declaring himself head of the Church in England and the break with Rome was complete. Over the next five years the land and wealth of the Church was subject to widespread confiscation, and in the process known as the Dissolution of the Monasteries most religious houses were closed, their buildings demolished and their monks turned out to fend for themselves.

THE WALK

❶ Starting with your back to the war memorial in front of St Peter and St Paul's church, walk passing the church on your left into the churchyard. Go ahead through a gate onto a grassy area, and go half left along a tarmac path, signed 'Country Walk'. Follow the path through a gate into the cemetery and immediately turn right. Follow the wall for 20 yards, then go through a kissing gate onto a track. Turn left along the track for 50 yards and then turn right through a kissing gate. Go diagonally across the corner of a field to another kissing gate on the far side. Follow the path down the next field to a kissing gate in the bottom right-hand corner. Go through the gate and follow the enclosed footpath, crossing over the river Blythe and continuing to eventually join a gravel track.

❷ Keep ahead along the track for ½ mile, ignoring two turns to the right (the second into a farm), eventually passing through a band of trees to reach a metal gate. Go through the gate onto a golf course and keep ahead, the fence close on your right. Follow the fence for 600 yards, to pass between lakes.

The golf course is on land that was previously part of the park that surrounded Maxstoke Castle, glimpses of which can be seen through the trees on your left. The castle was built around 1344 by Geoffrey de Clinton, who had served Edward III in the French Wars, holding the strategically important offices of Warden of the Cinque Ports and Constable of Dover Castle. He was rewarded in 1337 by being made Earl of Huntington. The de Clinton family had a long association with Warwickshire: the founder of the dynasty, William de Clinton, had built Kenilworth Castle (see walk 10), and over the generations strategic marriages had increased the family's estates in the county. Geoffrey de Clinton saw Maxstoke as the centre of the family's power and built an elaborate castle, a mile or so north of his existing manor house. The castle was completed around 1344, and in 1345 Huntington was given licence to crenellate (fortify) the castle.

Maxstoke was a perfectly symmetrical castle, with corner towers, a fortified gatehouse and high curtain walls, the whole being surrounded by a moat. It was built from local red sandstone, primarily as a residence rather than as a military stronghold. The main residential quarters were built around the interior courtyard. In 1437 the de Clintons did an exchange with the Earl of Stafford (later 1st Duke of Buckingham), swapping Maxstoke for estates in Northampton. The castle came briefly into royal hands, after the 2nd Duke of Buckingham was executed for rebelling against Richard III, and was in royal hands again after the 3rd Duke was executed for treason by Henry VIII. The castle passed through various owners before being acquired by

The gatehouse at Maxstoke Priory

Thomas Dilke in 1597, and it has remained in the Dilke family ever since. Although the interior buildings have been much altered over the centuries, the outer walls have remained largely unchanged, and today it is one of the most perfectly preserved 14th-century castles in England.

Maxstoke Castle is not open to the public except upon rare occasions.

Keep ahead, crossing the fairway with care and aiming just to the right of a stand of poplars ahead. Keep ahead across a second fairway, aiming for a sign board seen 20 yards to the right of a telephone pole. Go through the kissing gate ahead and continue along the side of a field, the hedge close on your left. After 200 yards cross a waymarked stile in the hedge on your left. Go half left across the golf course, passing close to a prominent oak seen ahead, to reach a kissing gate leading into a lane.

❸ Turn left along the lane for 50 yards, and then turn right through a gate and over a cattle grid onto a concrete drive. Follow the drive for over ½ mile. Some 100 yards short of the farm, at a gateway, go left over a stile, then go half left across the field. Once over the shallow rise ahead a stile comes into sight, at the right-hand end of woods ahead. Cross the stile and go along the side of a field, the woods close on your left. At the end of the field, ignore both a kissing gate on the left and a stile ahead, but turn right along the fence. Follow the field boundary, the fence close on your left, to reach a stile in the top corner of the field. Cross the stile, cross a track and a second stile, and then keep ahead along the field edge, the hedge close on your left.

In the far corner of the field cross a stile and then turn right, walking with the hedge now on your right. Cross a stile into the next field, turn left and follow the left-hand boundary to enter an enclosed track. Follow the track to cross a stile ahead, and then keep ahead along the enclosed footpath. After leaving the footpath maintain your direction to a kissing gate into a lane.

❹ Turn left along the lane. In 100 yards, just before a bend, go right through a kissing gate. Cross the corner of the field to a second kissing gate and then keep ahead to cross the huge field. A waymark post on an isolated tree in front marks the way, and as you proceed a second isolated, waymarked tree comes into sight. The path drops down to a gate in the bottom right-hand corner of the field. Follow the path through a band of trees and keep ahead along the next field, the hedge close on your right, to go through a gate in the far corner. Cross a footbridge and climb steps, then bear right to follow the right-hand edge of the field. Maintain your direction along the next field, the hedge still on your right, aiming for the church tower seen ahead. Go through a gate onto a road and turn right, passing the church and the wall of the old priory to the priory gatehouse.

The Augustinian priory at Maxstoke was founded in 1336 by Geoffrey de Clinton, the owner of substantial estates in Warwickshire which were controlled from nearby Maxstoke manor (soon to be replaced by the more imposing castle). It was not unusual for rich families to found religious houses in the Middle Ages. A whole range of reasons influenced them to do this. It was a time of genuine religious conviction, and many wealthy citizens truly desired to demonstrate their faith by helping the church. Not only did they wish to glorify God with imposing buildings, but they also wanted to use some of their wealth to support the work of the church. The additional benefit of endowing religious houses was that the monks or nuns would say regular prayers for their benefactor and his family.

The Augustinian order observed rules laid down by St Augustine, Bishop of Hippo. Unlike some other religious orders, the Augustinians went out preaching, spreading the word of God, and also concentrated upon helping their congregation with their physical needs, ministering to the poor and the sick. The Augustinians did not believe in living in the same degree of austerity as some other orders, and their religious houses were often comparatively luxurious.

Maxstoke Priory was one of the last Augustinian foundations opened in Warwickshire (the first was Kenilworth Priory, built by William, the first of the de Clinton barons). It was closed in 1538, its monks turned out to fare for themselves, and its assets sold off to local magnates. Much of its land was bought by Geoffrey de Clinton, the precious lead and glass confiscated from the priory, and the buildings dismantled for building materials. Today little remains apart from the imposing gatehouses (the outer one that faces onto the road and an inner one that has since been converted into a house) and some lengths of wall which have been incorporated into the subsequent farm.

❺   From the priory gatehouse, follow the lane around a bend and 100 yards later turn left into Arnolds Lane. Follow this quiet lane for 1¼ miles as it meanders between fields and hedgerows, to finally reach a T-junction. Turn left and follow the road over the bridge. On the far side of the bridge turn left down steps and then go through a kissing gate. Follow the riverside path for 250 yards. Where the river bends left, keep ahead across the embankment of a disused railway to a stile ahead.

❻   Follow the left-hand edge of the field to go through a kissing gate. Turn right along the edge of the field to another kissing gate beside a field gate seen ahead. Go through and turn left along the edge of a field, a fence and then a hedge on your left. Maintain your direction through a gap in the hedge and along the next field, the hedge now on your right, soon passing under power lines. In the corner of the field, turn right over a stile and go along the edge of the next field, the hedge now on your left.

In 50 yards go through a gap in the hedge and then go half right across the next field, aiming for houses on the far side. Go through a kissing gate and turn right along a track. Follow the track as it becomes an access road, with houses on your left, out to a main road. Cross the road and keep ahead along the tarmac track opposite. Follow the track through a gate into the cemetery. At the end of the wall on your left, bear left on a path back to the church and the start.

REFRESHMENTS

There are several pubs in Coleshill that offer a range of food. There are also shops, restaurants and sandwich bars.

WALK 8
SHAKESPEARE'S ROMANTIC STRATFORD

Length: 4 miles

The house in Henley Street where Shakespeare was born

HOW TO GET THERE: The walk starts from the Shakespeare Centre in Henley Street, Stratford upon Avon, which is 8 miles south-west from Warwick on the A439.

PARKING: There is ample pay-and-display parking in Stratford, and the Shakespeare Centre is signposted throughout the town.

MAP: OS Landranger 151 (GR 201551).

INTRODUCTION

A fascinating walk through the town of Stratford, enjoying sights associated with William Shakespeare and following the playwright's life and influence from birth to death and beyond. It is mainly on pavements and footpaths, with no gradients, and route-finding is easy.

HISTORICAL BACKGROUND

Although Stratford upon Avon has been a significant settlement for a thousand years, its name is universally associated with just one of its citizens, William Shakespeare.

There is evidence that since the Bronze Age, 2000 BC, there has been a settlement in the vicinity of modern Stratford, where the fast-flowing river Avon could be forded. The Roman road, Icknield Street, leading from the salt-mines of Droitwich to the Thames valley and hence eventually to London, crossed the river here, thus providing the Saxons with their name for the town – where the road or 'street' fords the Avon.

By the end of the 13th century Stratford had become a thriving town, the centre of trade and commerce in the area, with a three-day market held monthly. To the north and east of the town was the vast Forest of Arden, covering a huge swathe of the Midlands, home to many small hamlets whose inhabitants eked out a living in the woods. To the south and east, now linked to Stratford by a sturdy wooden bridge, were the rich farmlands of the Feldon. The population of the town grew, with tradesmen supplying the farmers and the foresters, and merchants handling the growing trade. It became dominated by the Guild of the Holy Trinity, a religious body devoted to providing both physical and spiritual help to the town.

In 1557 John Shakespeare, originally a yeoman farmer in nearby Snitterfield, improved his fortunes by marrying Mary, the daughter and heiress of his landlord

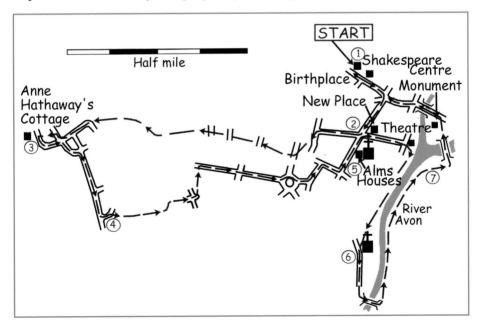

Robert Arden. Shakespeare had moved into Stratford, set up a profitable business as a general tradesman, and soon rose through a series of civic offices to become bailiff (the equivalent of mayor) of Stratford in 1568. His oldest son, William, was born in 1564.

In 1582, the 18-year-old William hastily married Anne Hathaway, a bare three months before she bore their first child. The next few years are shrouded in obscurity. Shakespeare supported his growing family with various jobs, possibly including teaching, maybe working as a lawyer's clerk. Sometime between 1585 and 1588, Shakespeare left Stratford. He moved to London, where he gained employment in the theatre, graduating via acting to editing and rewriting other people's plays before finally trying his hand at writing. When *Henry VI Part I* was produced in 1592 it was clear that a major new talent had arrived on the London theatre scene, a talent which would grow from strength to strength to become arguably the world's greatest playwright. In the process his birthplace, Stratford, would be immortalized.

THE WALK

❶ With your back to the Shakespeare Centre, turn left and walk past Shakespeare's Birthplace.

John Shakespeare had moved from his farm in Snitterfield to this property in Henley Street in 1552. After his advantageous marriage to Mary Arden in 1557, he extended and improved the house. The original property consisted of two houses, surrounded by a garden and paddock. One house was the family home, now extended as the family grew by the addition of another wing. The second house was used by John as his shop. A yeoman farmer whilst at Snitterfield, once he moved to Stratford he became a trader, dealing in malt, corn, leather, hides and wool. He later diversified further, by becoming both a glove seller and a retail butcher.

With increased wealth John received a series of offices in Stratford, commencing as ale-taster (responsible for the quality of ale) in 1557, progressing through alderman in 1565, to become bailiff or mayor in 1568. He and Mary had eight children in all: firstly two girls, both of whom died in infancy, then his first son William in 1564, followed by three more sons and two more daughters. John's fortunes failed in 1576, when he fell into debt. He largely withdrew from public life, stopped attending church for fear of arrest, and borrowed increasingly large amounts of money from his Arden relatives, resulting in the sale or mortgage of most of Mary Arden's inheritance. A heavy fine in 1580 almost ruined him.

It was against this background that William grew up. Initially the son of a prosperous and influential citizen, he received a good education at the local grammar school. Even as a boy he helped his father in his various businesses, and with his father's near ruin when William was 16 he was forced into working full time with his father to help obviate the family's declining fortunes.

Shakespeare's birthplace is open daily; times vary dependent upon the time of year. Admission charge.

Continue along the road to reach a mini-roundabout, with the wide Market Street in front of you.

Market Street was the original market square and was the heart of medieval Stratford. The town's daily retail business was conducted from the shops and stalls that lined the square. A market was held once a month, for three consecutive days, when the farmers and herdsmen from the surrounding countryside brought their produce to market, and traders from as far away as London came to sell their wares. The charter to hold this market was the basis of the town's prosperity, for not only did it allow Stratford to host a market but it also forbade any other town within 7 miles to hold one, thereby ensuring that Stratford grew as a regional commercial centre. Fires in 1594 and 1595 destroyed many of the old houses in Stratford, and most of the buildings around the square were built after that time. Shakespeare drew inspiration for his writing not only from books and classical texts, but also from his acute observations of everyday life. Memories of the bustling street markets of his youth feature in the crowd scenes that come so vividly to life in his plays.

Turn right (currently, across the front of Barclays Bank). Cross the road and keep ahead along High Street (WH Smith's on the left-hand side of the road).

High Street is lined with many half-timbered buildings that survived the various fires which were such a great threat to medieval towns, full as they were of overcrowded wooden buildings. These date from Shakespeare's day, and would have been familiar to him.

Cross a side road (Ely Street) and keep ahead to the church in front of you.

This beautiful church was built as the chapel of the Guild of Holy Cross, beyond which was the half-timbered guildhall, today almshouses. The Guild of Holy Cross dominated medieval Stratford and all the prosperous members of the community, including John Shakespeare, sought to belong to it. Although it was a religious order, it also involved itself in looking after the secular needs of its members. It provided education for the children, a hospital, a rudimentary welfare benefit in times of hardship, and a form of unemployment benefit, as well as holding normal church services and saying prayers for the souls of departed guild members.

On the first floor above the guildhall was a schoolroom, where the Guild ran a grammar school open to the children of all members. William Shakespeare was enrolled in this school at the age of seven. The emphasis was upon Latin grammar, the language of the professional classes, although during the course of his education, subjects such as classical literature, philosophy, history and rhetoric would also have been studied. Contrary to popular myth, Shakespeare was not self-taught. Rather, he had an in-depth education lasting many years under a number of highly successful teachers. The works he studied provided the plots for many of his plays, whilst the formal discipline of rhetoric, as well as the classical poetry he studied, comes through in his verse.

During the Dissolution of the Monasteries the Guild of Holy Cross was closed down, and in 1553 its property was given to the newly formed Borough of Stratford upon Avon. The guildhall was turned into almshouses to support the poor of the town, the chapel was given to the Borough as a church, and the schooling function taken over by the newly created King Edward VI Grammar School, housed in specially built schoolrooms in the guildhall grounds.

② Opposite the church, turn right along Scholars Lane and follow it to its end. Cross the main road half right and enter the small gardens in front of you. Turn left along the central path to exit in the top right corner. Cross the road and turn left. Immediately past the Woodstock Guest House, turn right into an alley, signed to 'Anne Hathaway's Cottage'.

Anne Hathaway's Cottage stands in Shottery, today a suburb of Stratford but in Shakespeare's day a separate village. This alley follows an old path that would have led out of Stratford and through the fields to Shottery, one of the many paths Shakespeare would have been familiar with.

Follow the alley, crossing a cycle path and keeping ahead along an enclosed footpath for 30 yards, to cross a road. Keep ahead along the enclosed footpath and follow it across two more roads, then over a stream, and then across a green open space. On the far side of the green continue along an enclosed footpath, a school on your left. At a fork in 50 yards, keep ahead, signed 'Anne Hathaway's Cottage via Tavern Lane'. Follow the footpath out to the corner of a lane and keep ahead along the lane. At a T-junction, keep ahead for 20 yards to a crossroads.

This is the centre of Shottery, a tiny hamlet on the borders of the Forest of Arden, once a huge forest that covered most of the Midlands, and still in Shakespeare's day covering all of north and west Warwickshire, as well as much of Staffordshire and a substantial portion of Worcestershire. The forest was not continuous: rather it consisted of stretches of dense woodland interspersed with less thickly forested areas, and glades in which were isolated dwellings and small hamlets. The forest appears in several of Shakespeare's plays, explicitly in As You Like It, *and as the inspiration for the magical woods in* A Midsummer Night's Dream.

Cross the road half right and go up steps. Keep ahead along the footpath, a field on your right. Follow the footpath over a bridge and out to a lane opposite Anne Hathaway's Cottage.

Hewlands Farm was home to Richard Hathaway, whose family in 1582 included his daughter Anne, then 25 and, unusually for that time, unmarried. She was courted by the 18-year-old William Shakespeare, whether out of passion or because she was heiress to a comfortably off yeoman farmer is uncertain. By August 1582 it was becoming evident that the spinster Anne was pregnant, and two of Hathaway's neighbours arranged for a special licence to be granted by the Bishop of Worcester, allowing a marriage to be hurried through without awaiting the reading of the usual church banns. In November 1582 William and Anne were married, and moved in with John Shakespeare at the Henley Street house. Three months later Anne gave birth to the couple's first daughter, Susanna.

Shakespeare took up various employments to support his wife and growing family: Susanna was joined by twins in 1585. The marriage does not appear to have been an especially happy one, and it is likely that the artistically inclined Shakespeare felt trapped in a hum-drum existence. Sometime between 1585 and 1588 Shakespeare suddenly left Stratford, his wife and young family, to go to London. He was not to see them again for two years, and even after that, only during fleeting annual returns to his native town. Once Stratford became gripped by 'Shakespeare mania', Hewlands Farm was renamed Anne Hathaway's Cottage. It is little altered from Anne's day.

Open daily, times vary dependent upon the time of year. Admission charge.

❸ With your back to the cottage turn right along the lane, turning left with the lane to return to the crossroads. Turn right along Shottery, passing the Bell on your left and the Santa Lucia restaurant on your right, and then turning right into a suburban lane. Cross the road opposite St Andrew's School and continue along the lane. Cross Quineys Road and keep ahead. Turn left along Seymour Road. Where Seymour Road turns left, keep ahead along a track.

❹ Follow the track past the backs of houses. At a T-junction in front of sheds, turn left and then follow the track around to the right, resuming your previous direction. Follow the track out to the apparent end of a cul de sac. Keep ahead for 20 yards, to the end of the road. Turn left into a footpath, to the right of 'Brownlow Drive 19-25'. Follow the footpath out to a road and turn right, to reach a roundabout. Go left around the roundabout, crossing a main road and then turning into Broad Walk. In 100 yards, at a cross road, turn left along Broad Street. Pass a school on your left and at a T-junction, turn right.

❺ In 200 yards turn left into Church Street and follow the road, passing almshouses on the right. You are now back at the guildhall of the Guild of Holy Cross. Continue past the church and turn right. On the opposite side of the road, beyond the wall, are the remains of New Place.

By 1587 Shakespeare had become one of England's most sought-after playwrights. He had a dozen plays to his credit, ranging from comedies such as The Taming of the Shrew *and* A Midsummer Night's Dream, *to histories such as* Henry VI, Richard II *and* King John, *and gory tragedies like* Titus Andronicus. *He had become very wealthy and returned to Stratford in that year to clear his father's debts. He also bought New Place, the largest house in town, which was to become his home until his death. He stayed in New Place during his annual visits to Stratford, and he retired to here in 1610.*

The house was huge, with five gables and a courtyard as well as an extensive garden. It was demolished in the 18th century, and all that remains today are the gardens and part of the foundations. Next door to New Place is Nash's House, a contemporary building that was home to Shakespeare's granddaughter, Elizabeth and her husband, Thomas Nash.

Nash's House and New Place (which is entered through Nash's House) are open daily, times vary dependent upon time of year. Admission charge.

Follow the road past King Edward's Grammar School.

This school was founded in 1553 by King Edward VI and replaced the grammar school run by the Guild of Holy Cross. New school rooms were built in the guildhall grounds, but have long since been demolished and replaced by the modern structure.

At a T-junction in front of the theatre, turn right. Cross the road and enter a footpath to the right of the theatre. Turn right with the footpath along the river bank, soon walking parallel with the road again.

Where you join the road is the famous public house, the Black Swan/Dirty Duck. Its sign has both names, one each side of the signboard, and they are meant to reflect the clientele. Coming from the town side, the sign reads the genteel 'Black Swan': from the theatre, where disreputable actors are likely to come for refreshment, it is named the 'Dirty Duck'.

Follow the footpath past a foot ferry, past the brass rubbing centre, and eventually swinging right to the road. Turn left along the road to reach the path leading into Holy Trinity church.

The church of Holy Trinity stood outside the boundaries of Shakespeare's Stratford, on the site of a Saxon monastery. With the Dissolution of the Monasteries and the later creation of the Borough of Stratford, it became the parish church of the town. Shakespeare and Anne Hathaway were married in this church in 1583, and their children Susanna and the twins Hamnet and Judith were christened here.

After his acquisition of New Place in 1587, Shakespeare returned to Stratford at roughly yearly intervals, and steadily increased his holdings in the town. In 1602 he bought 100 acres of arable land and 20 acres of pasture from the Clopton family, leading citizens in the town. The following year he bought a cottage adjoining New Place, and in 1605 he bought up several local tithes, which provided a steady income from rent. All of this he could afford due to the huge success of his plays, produced by his own stage company. He had highly influential patrons, such as the Earl of Essex, and his works were greatly admired by Queen Elizabeth herself. During this period Shakespeare created his greatest masterpieces, works such as Hamlet, Macbeth, Othello *and the mighty* King Lear, *works unequalled by any playwright before or since. In 1610 Shakespeare wrote his last great play,* The Tempest, *generally assumed to be his swansong, and retired to New Place. He died there on St George's Day, 23 April 1616, and was buried in Holy Trinity church.*

Open daily; times vary according to time of year. Free admission.

6 Follow the path, passing the church on your left, to reach the road again. Keep ahead along the road, a high wall on your left. At the end of the road, keep ahead along a walled footpath to reach a footbridge over the river Avon. Turn left over the footbridge. On the far side turn left again and follow the riverside path, looking across to Holy Trinity church, to reach the Shakespeare Theatre on the opposite bank.

Shakespeare had constantly adapted to changing fashions in the theatre, and his later works reflected the changes in stagecraft that were to become prevalent in the Jacobean theatre. After his death his works remained popular. They were regularly staged in London and elsewhere, but it was not until 1746 that any of Shakespeare's plays were produced in Stratford. In 1769 the actor David Garrick held a Shakespeare Festival here, but even then no regular production of his works took place in his home town. It was not until 1879 that the first Memorial Theatre was opened and Shakespeare's plays have been performed here ever since. The present theatre was built in 1932, and was extensively restored in 2008.

7 Follow the path, past a café on the right and a boat club on the left, to reach a road. Immediately turn left and go over the stone footbridge back over the Avon.

To your right is the Clopton Bridge, a 22-arch stone bridge built across the Avon to replace the previous wooden structure. It was paid for by John Clopton, the town's richest merchant and landowner, who had also built the Guild Chapel at Holy Cross and sold land to Shakespeare.

Follow the footpath out to the main road and turn left, passing the Gower Monument.

The Gower Monument was erected in 1888 in the Memorial Gardens, adjacent to the theatre, and moved to its present location in 1933. The main statue is of Shakespeare, and at each corner is one of his greatest creations – Hamlet, Falstaff, Henry V *and* Macbeth. *It was raised to commemorate Stratford's most famous son, and it seems fitting that, after seeing the buildings associated with his life, we should see this memorial to his literary legacy.*

Follow the pavement over the bridge. Cross a side road and keep ahead up the shopping street. In front of WH Smith, cross the road at traffic lights and turn left. Cross a side road and keep ahead, Barclays Bank on your left, to return to the Shakespeare Centre.

WALK 9

CHARLECOTE HOUSE AND THE ELIZABETHAN COUNTRYSIDE

Length: 6 miles

Charlecote House, now in the care of the National Trust

HOW TO GET THERE: The walk starts from the gates of Charlecote Park. Charlecote is 1 mile from Wellesbourne, on the B4088, which joins the A429 Warwick to Wellesbourne road.

PARKING: There is a large National Trust car park, free to members. Alternatively, there is a large lay-by in front of the church, 100 yards from the gates of Charlecote Park, where there is ample parking on most occasions.

MAP: OS Landranger 151 (GR 264563).

INTRODUCTION

Charlecote's fine Tudor manor house makes an impressive start to this walk, which goes past Charlecote mill and along river bluffs above the river Avon before returning via the pretty village of Hampton Lucy. It is mainly on field paths, with occasional stretches of quiet country lane, with few gradients and easy route-finding.

HISTORICAL BACKGROUND

In the 16th century Warwickshire was quintessentially rural England, dominated by neither grand nobility nor a strong merchant class. Instead, social and political power lay with its rural gentry, typical of whom were the Lucy family of Charlecote.

The Lucy family had lived at Charlecote since the 12th century, although they did not adopt the name Lucy until the 13th century. Thomas Lucy inherited the estate in 1551, added to it lands acquired from the recently suppressed friary of Thelsford, and also enlarged it with the dowry of his rich wife, Joyce Acton. Lucy owned large estates around Stratford, and as one of the district's richest citizens exerted considerable power, not only in his role as landlord but also by holding a number of public offices. He became the Sheriff of Warwickshire and also one of the county's Members of Parliament, using his power as a major local landowner to simply instruct the electors to vote him into office. Lucy was knighted in 1565, and such was his prestige that in 1572 Queen Elizabeth herself stayed for two days at Charlecote Park whilst en route to visiting the Earl of Leicester at Kenilworth (see walk 10). Throughout his life Sir Thomas continued to enlarge his fortune, increasing the income of his Charlecote estates by enclosing land for sheep farming, and also from judicial investment in the burgeoning trades based in Stratford. He was very cognizant of the law, and was ever willing to take neighbours and tenants to court to preserve and extend his wealth and property. When he died in 1600 his son, Thomas Lucy II, inherited not only a substantial fortune but also a position of power within the county.

The influence that Sir Thomas had accrued served the family well in succeeding generations. Although Sir Thomas' great-grandson Spenser fought for the losing side during the Civil War, the family saved Charlecote from confiscation by a mixture of bribes and calling in favours from their neighbours. The Lucys remained squires of Charlecote for many generations, and exerted a controlling influence over the affairs of the district until well into the 19th century. Charlecote remains the home of the Lucy family.

THE WALK

❶ The walk starts from the gates of Charlecote Park, from where there is a good view of the house, standing proudly at the end of the drive.

Thomas Lucy set about building Charlecote House in the early 1550s, and work was completed around 1559. Its plan was typical of many country houses of that period. A main two-storey block containing a great hall and gallery is flanked by two projecting

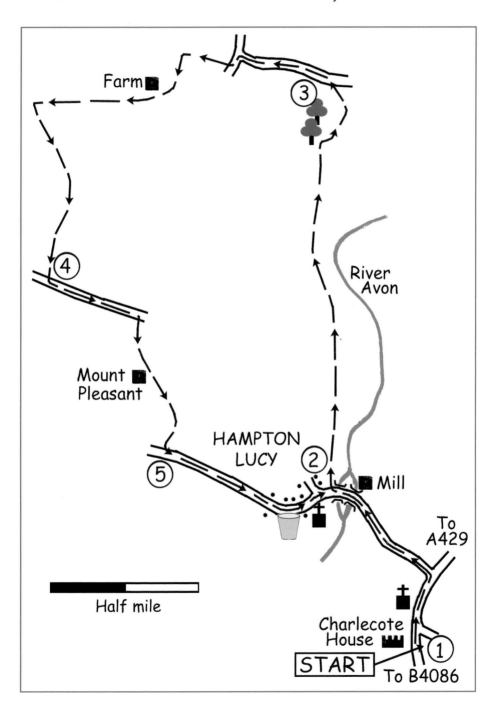

Farm

③

River
Avon

④

Mount
Pleasant

HAMPTON
LUCY

⑤

②

Mill

To
A429

Half mile

Charlecote
House

START

①

To B4086

wings which envelop an entrance yard. An elaborate porch leads from the yard into the centre of the main building. It has a regular and symmetrical façade, with the elaborate chimneys and gables typical of Tudor architecture, the whole being built in the classic red brick of the period. Behind the main building are outbuildings, including a stable and a brewery, whilst in front, beyond a walled forecourt, is a free-standing two-storey gatehouse. The whole building echoes in its design the walled defensive manor houses of earlier years, but its defences are all for show, decorations upon a house built specifically as the grand but comfortable home of a local magnate.

Formal gardens were laid out behind the house in the late 17th century, but these were totally redesigned in 1760 by the most famous landscape gardener of his day, 'Capability' Brown. Brown, whose trademark design was a stylised improvement upon nature, widened the river Avon behind the house, levelling the banks and creating a waterfall, and replaced the formal gardens with sweeping lawns that dropped down to the river. Although the interior of the house was transformed in the 18th and 19th centuries, the Elizabethan exterior has been largely retained, and the Charlecote we see today has changed remarkably little since it was built by Thomas Lucy.

Charlecote House is open from 1st March until the end of October, 12 noon to 5 pm, daily apart from Wednesday and Thursday: the park is open all year round, 10.30 am to 4 pm (6 pm March to October). There is an admission charge; free to National Trust members.

With your back to the entrance gates of Charlecote Park, turn left along the road, soon passing St Leonard's church.

There has been a church here since 1187, when a small Anglo-Norman building was raised in a grove of trees. When Sir Thomas Lucy died in 1600, he was buried with considerable pomp and ceremony in this church, interred in a magnificent alabaster tomb alongside his wife, who had died five years earlier. His tomb, together with those of his son and grandson, can still be seen in the church. The church building evolved over time, but remained small and unelaborated, and in 1853 it was totally rebuilt as the Victorian edifice seen today.

A wicket gate at the rear of the church provides entry from the house and park into the church grounds. Although you cannot now go the other way through the gate, it does afford a good view over the deer park towards Charlecote House.

The first deer park was enclosed here in 1477. After Charlecote House was completed the deer park was expanded, where Sir Thomas and his guests could hunt the herd of fallow deer especially imported to stock the park. Red deer were introduced in 1845 by Henry Lucy, and there are still some 150 red deer and 250 fallow deer, descendants of those Lucy herds, roaming the park today.

There is a legend that the young William Shakespeare was caught poaching deer in this park in 1583, and rather than face prosecution in front of the local magistrate (Sir Thomas Lucy himself) he fled to London. There is no evidence whatsoever to support this story, and it is most likely Shakespeare simply left parochial Stratford to pursue his fortune in the capital (see walk 8). Sir Thomas Lucy would have been well known to Shakespeare and did provide the model for the fussy Justice Shallow, the object of fun in Henry IV Part II *and* The Merry Wives of Windsor, *but the undoubted contempt the playwright felt for a local dignitary does not prove any personal involvement.*

Continue past the church and in 300 yards turn left into a side road. Follow this lane, a pavement on the right-hand side, to reach the river Avon and the watermill.

From Saxon times onwards, villagers in rural England had existed at little above subsistence level. The most valuable tools and resources, such as ploughs or the teams of oxen needed to draw them, were beyond the means of most villagers to possess. Instead, they were owned by a few rich individuals, who then rented them out. The most valuable and lucrative resource for any village was a mill, for although villagers grew their own corn, it still had to be ground into flour. The local landlord often owned the mill, which he rented out to a miller in return for a percentage of the miller's takings. It was frequently written into the tenancy agreement of villagers that they had to use the landlord's mill, at non-negotiable prices. In addition, the miller often took advantage of his monopoly to put his own percentage on top of the landlord's fee. In consequence, the miller was often one of the most loathed men in the community.

There has been a mill here on the river Avon since at least 1086, the property of the landlord of the estate, renting out its services to the villagers around. Mills, being wooden structures which contained spark-producing grindstones, were prone to burning down, and the original Charlecote Mill has long since gone. The present mill was built in 1806 by Sir Edmund Fairfax Lucy, and has been little altered to the present day.

Charlecote Mill is open the first Sunday of the month, April to October, and also bank holidays. There is an entrance charge.

Follow the lane for another 100 yards to cross a second bridge.

You are now on the outskirts of the village of Hampton Lucy. In the Middle Ages the village was part of the feudal holdings of the Bishop of Worcester, and was called Bishops Hampton. After the Dissolution of the Monasteries the land was acquired by Thomas Lucy, who changed the name of the village to reflect its new owner. Although the old feudal relationship of master and serf had long since gone, Lucy continued to be very much the master of the estate, enclosing some of the common land around the village for his own estates, and insisting upon full and prompt payment of rents from the villagers, upon pain of eviction. Lucy frequently resorted to the law to fine or even expel recalcitrant tenants, recourse undoubtedly aided by the fact that he was the local magistrate.

➋ Immediately over the bridge, turn right down a tarmac drive. Follow the drive to a gate and turn left up a waymarked footpath. Follow the enclosed footpath through a gate and keep ahead on a clear path through shrubland to a second gate leading into a field. Keep ahead along the side of the field, hedgerow close on your right. In 200 yards go right through a gate and follow a path, parallel to the field boundary. Follow the path along the top of river bluffs before going left through a gate back into the field. Maintain your direction along the side of the field. Follow the path along a second field, meandering along with the hedge close on your right. Follow the path into a third field and now keep ahead along a line of trees, diverging away from the hedge on your right.

Where the line of trees ends, keep ahead on a clear path over the field, soon to reach the corner of shrubland on the right. Turn right here and walk downhill, the shrubland on your left. In 80 yards turn right through a gap in the hedge and walk with the shrubland on your left and a new plantation on your right. Where the plantation ends keep ahead, shrubland still on the left. At the end of the field, go ahead into the next field and then bear left on a grassy path, a second new plantation soon on your right.

➌ Follow the path out to a lane and turn left. Follow the lane for 400 yards to a T-junction. Go half left across the lane to a waymarked stile in the hedge ahead. Keep ahead along the field, the hedge close on your left. In 200 yards pass a gate and 30 yards later, turn left over a stile beside a second gate. Follow the bottom edge of the field, a fence on your left. In the field corner turn right and follow the boundary fence for 40 yards to cross a stile on your left. Go half right across the corner of the field to a pedestrian gate leading onto a drive. Cross the drive and go through the gate opposite, and follow the hedge to a second gate 20 yards ahead.

Keep ahead, the fence close on your right. Where the fence swings left, go right through a pedestrian gate and then resume your previous direction down a broad grassy track, the hedge close on your left. In the bottom corner of the field go over a stile ahead, to the right of the inviting field gate, and maintain your direction up the next field, the hedge still on your left. At the corner of the hedge turn left at a waymark post. Follow the boundary of this huge field, the hedge always close on your left, to reach a lane.

➍ Turn left along the lane for 600 yards, then turn right along the gravel drive to Mount Pleasant. Where the drive swings right to the house, keep ahead, soon with a hedge on your left. Follow the field boundary until it curves right, at which point keep a look-out for a waymarked stile in the hedge on your left. Cross the stile and resume your previous direction, the hedge now on your right. Follow the hedge to a lane.

❺ Turn left and follow the lane into the village of Hampton Lucy. Pass the Boars Head and then the church, standing back from the small village green.

The post of vicar of the church of St Peter Ad Vincula was traditionally given to a younger son of the Lucy family, a practice that prevailed until well into the 19th century. This was common in rural England, where estates passed to the eldest son, and the local church was used to provide a living for one of the younger sons. The fact that these sons had no theological training was no bar, since they rarely conducted any services or other church functions, but instead employed a verger to undertake the actual work of the parish for a pittance. The Lucy connection did benefit the church here in Hampton Lucy in 1822, when the 122 ft high tower was added, in order to enhance the view from Charlecote House across the park, where the new church tower now provided a pleasing backdrop.

Follow the road round to the left to a T-junction. Turn right and follow the lane over the river, past the mill and back to the main road at Charlecote. Turn right back to the start.

WALK 10

KENILWORTH CASTLE: THE QUEEN AND THE COURTIER

Length: 4 miles

The ruins of Kenilworth Castle

HOW TO GET THERE: Kenilworth is on the A452, 4 miles north of Leamington Spa. The walk starts from Abbey Fields car park in the centre of the town.

PARKING: Abbey Fields car park is on the north-eastern side of the common, clearly signposted.

MAP: OS Landranger 140 (GR 286724).

INTRODUCTION

This walk starts in the heart of Kenilworth, going through the grounds of the abbey, then passing the castle and the attractive lake. It crosses fields and skirts woods to return to Kenilworth and the abbey ruins. Route-finding is simple, terrain is easy and there are no gradients.

HISTORICAL BACKGROUND

Today Kenilworth Castle is a romantic ruin, but four centuries ago it was the backdrop to one of the great romances in English history, the love affair between Queen Elizabeth I and Robert Dudley, Earl of Leicester.

When Elizabeth ascended the throne in 1558 she was 25 years old, and the most eligible unmarried woman in Europe. To her ministers, the pressing question of the new reign was who the queen would take for a husband. For Elizabeth faced the same problem that had beset her father Henry VIII, namely securing the dynasty by producing an undisputed heir to whom the throne would pass. Elizabeth was not short of suitors amongst the royalty of Europe, or alternatively she could look amongst her own subjects for a husband. Marriage, however, presented problems for Elizabeth. If she choose a foreign prince from either Catholic or Protestant camp she offended the other, and severely limited her flexibility in foreign policy. Marriage to one of her subjects risked creating domestic factionalism. Taking any husband, in the male-dominated world of the 16th century, risked restricting her freedom to rule as she wished.

Although in the first two years of her reign Elizabeth politely listened to many suitors, the one thought most likely to be successful was Robert Dudley, son of the Duke of Northumberland who had been executed for his plot to usurp Queen Mary. Princess Elizabeth and Robert Dudley had met as teenagers at the court of her brother Edward VI and fallen in love. Both had been imprisoned in the Tower during Mary's reign. On her accession Elizabeth appointed Dudley as her Master of Horse, and it seemed obvious to her ministers that they were infatuated with each other, despite the fact that Dudley already had a wife. Marriage seemed a strong possibility, to the alarm of her more conservative ministers, who mistrusted the flamboyant and impetuous Dudley.

The suspicious death of Dudley's wife cleared the way for marriage to the Queen, but cast such a cloud of suspicion that marriage was made impossible. For

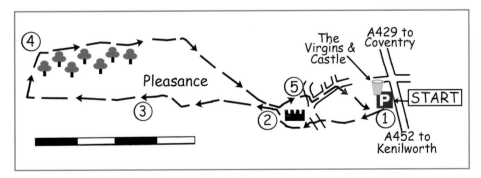

the next ten years Elizabeth entertained many potential suitors, but all were politely refused. Whether she ever intended marriage, or whether the possibility of marriage was being used as a diplomatic bargaining tool, is a matter of debate. It seems clear, however, that Elizabeth remained in love with Dudley throughout her life, and he never lost hope of marrying her. In 1575 he made his last serious bid to win the Queen, and Kenilworth Castle was the setting for that attempt.

THE WALK

❶ With your back to the car park entrance, go along the tarmac path, past the tennis courts.

This park is called Abbey Fields, after the abbey which stood here. The few remaining ruins of the abbey can be seen on your right, whilst the land in front was its gardens and pastures. The Priory of St Mary was founded in 1124 by Geoffrey de Clinton, for canons of the Augustinian order. De Clinton and later patrons gave the priory extensive estates in Kenilworth and elsewhere, and over time it became one of Warwickshire's richest landowners, rising to become the largest religious house in the county. To reflect its growing status, the priory was made into an abbey by the Pope in 1447. It was signed over to the Crown in 1538 during the Dissolution of the Monasteries, its buildings dismantled for building stone. By 1600 little trace of the abbey remained.

Pass the swimming pool on your left and keep ahead to reach the lake. Follow the tarmac path along the side of the lake.

This lake is on the site of the old abbey pool, which was created by the canons of St Mary's to provide fish. After the Dissolution, the fishpond silted up over time until it had virtually disappeared. The present lake was recreated by the District Council in the 1990s.

Follow the path through a barrier and out on to the road. Turn left along the pavement. Where the railings end, cross the road and go through a gate in the wooden fence opposite. Bear left and follow the path as it winds through trees.

The ramparts to your left were the banks which created ponds of water to defend the southern approaches to the castle. A huge artificial lake stretched for a kilometre to the west, connected to a wide pool on your right which in turn drained into the abbey pool. Together they provided an impassable barrier on three sides of the castle. The ramparts were called 'the brays', a corruption of the word 'bay' or dock. In the medieval castle, the top of the brays was used as a tiltyard. The pool on the right was drained in the 16th century.

Go under the bridge. Keep ahead to the fence for a fine view of the castle and the site of the mere.

Around 1122 King Henry I granted Kenilworth to his chamberlain Geoffrey de Clinton, who divided the riverside estate into two parts. In the downstream part he endowed the priory that we have already seen, whilst upstream he built a castle, probably a simple motte and bailey (a keep on an earthen mound surrounded by a walled courtyard).

Over successive centuries the castle's size and defences were improved: the motte was topped with a masonry keep between 1150 and 1175 by Geoffrey's son, completed just in time to be held as a garrison for Henry II, when certain of his nobles rebelled against him. The castle was taken into royal hands during the reign of King John, at which time its main defences were completed: a high stone curtain wall was built, and a mere or lake was created on the west and southerly sides of the castle (the fields in front of you) to form an impassable barrier. In 1254 Kenilworth Castle passed into the hands of Simon de Montfort, Earl of Leicester, who further increased its fortifications. Kenilworth was central to his revolt against Henry III, during which it was besieged by royalist forces (see walk 5 for more on the Barons' Revolt). In the 13th century the castle passed to the Earls and Dukes of Lancaster, and in 1326 Edward II was imprisoned here until he abdicated in favour of his son. A later Duke of Lancaster, John of Gaunt, built the Great Hall and adjoining buildings.

In 1554 the castle was granted to John Dudley, Duke of Northumberland, shortly afterwards executed for his failed attempt to usurp Queen Mary and place Lady Jane Grey on the throne. After her accession Queen Elizabeth restored the Dudley fortunes: in 1563 Kenilworth was granted to Dudley's son Robert, who was also made Earl of Leicester. Robert Dudley built the towered gatehouse and other buildings. Queen Elizabeth stayed at Kenilworth three times, and her final visit, between the 9th and 25th July 1575, saw Dudley's final attempt to persuade the Queen to marry him. Lavish entertainments were laid on, including hunting, fireworks, displays in the tiltyard, and a boating trip upon the lake.

To visit the castle turn left, then left again over the bridge you have just passed beneath. To continue the walk, turn right along a track beside the causeway.

On your right is the causeway, which carried a roadway from the outer gatehouse to the main castle gate, and which dammed Finham brook to create the mere, or artificial lake. Originally a narrow crenellated roadway, it limited approach to the castle and added another layer of defence. By Tudor times defence was less of an issue, and the castle was used more as a stately home. Under Robert Dudley the causeway was widened so that it could be used as a tiltyard for jousting.

❷ Follow the path through a kissing gate and bear left beneath the walls of the castle.

The flat land on your left was once the large artificial lake or 'mere' that surrounded Kenilworth Castle on its western and southern sides, stretching for nearly a mile to the west.

Follow the path to a gate at the end of the hedge ahead, visible to the left of a pink-painted house. Go through the gate and turn left along a track for 500 yards, to the gates of High House Farm. Take the path to the right of the gates. Follow this enclosed path to a kissing gate. The earthworks in the field ahead of you are the remains of the Pleasance.

The Pleasance was built as a pleasure house by Henry V. It was a huge earthwork, as large as the castle itself, with a wooden wall enclosing pavilions. It had a double moat fed by the mere, on whose banks it stood, and it had its own dock on the mereside. King Henry enjoyed it as a pleasant retreat from the daily bustle in the castle, and successive owners used it as a place to provide entertainments for guests. Parties would be rowed across the lake from the castle and treated to elaborate picnics. The Pleasance also provided a base for hunting in the woods to the west, and doubtless featured in Dudley's entertainment of Queen Elizabeth in 1575.

From the gate go half left through the earthworks, aiming for a metal gate and waymark post in the hedge half ahead.

The Pleasance was to your right, and the remains of the moat around it can be seen as a ditch which still floods in wet weather. To your left was an outer wall, between the moated Pleasance and the mere. A dock coming in from the mere is in front of you.

❸ Cross a track and go through a kissing gate. Follow the path along the left-hand side of the field to a kissing gate in the corner. Go through the gate and keep ahead along the next field, the hedge now on your right, to cross a footbridge at the far end.

The footbridge crosses a ditch, now flooded, known as the Park Pale. This marked the boundary of the domesticated parkland that surrounded the Tudor castle: beyond it were open forests, outlying remains of the great Forest of Arden, suitable for hunting.

Keep ahead along the side of two more large fields. At the end of the second field, at a waymark post, turn right along a track. Climb with the track, a wood soon on your right, to reach a T-junction.

❹ Turn right along the tarmac track and follow it for ½ mile. Pass houses and garages on your left and continue along the track. In another 250 yards pass the drive to Pleasance Farm on your right. After 350 yards, opposite houses on the left, turn right through a kissing gate at a finger-post. Go half left across the field. On the far side go through a kissing gate and then turn left along the left edge of a field for 20 yards to go through a second kissing gate. Go through a band of trees and then keep ahead across the next three fields.

Fine views of the castle open up ahead of you. Remember that when it was built the mere would have stretched across the land in front of you, making the castle virtually impregnable from this side.

At the end of the third field go through a kissing gate and turn left along a track. Pass a pink cottage on your right and keep head along the track to reach the main road.

On your left was a deep moat, dug to let in water from the mere and protect the castle's northern wall. Between them, the moat and mere blocked access to the castle on all but its eastern side.

5 Turn right down the road.

On your right is the great Tudor gatehouse, built by Robert Dudley. Previously there had only been a postern gate here, with the main entrance coming in from the south-east, across the causeway. As defence became less of an issue, Dudley was able to dispense with the old entrance and create a more convenient and prestigious one. Dudley also created a knot garden to the west of the gatehouse, now restored.

At a green triangle, the Queen and Castle on your left, turn left along the road, soon passing the Clarendon Arms.

Pub names are a fascinating window onto local history. The Queen and Castle is self-evident, reflecting the visit of Queen Elizabeth in 1575. In 1611 Kenilworth Castle was seized by the Crown, and after the Restoration Charles II granted it to Thomas Villers, Earl of Clarendon. The Clarendon name turns up in a number of locations in Kenilworth, including this pub.

Cross Elizabeth Way and Malthouse Lane on the left, and then cross over the road and take a path off on the right leading into Abbey Fields. Follow the tarmac path down to an elaborate archway on your left.

This was the original archway of the Tantara gatehouse, built between 1361 and 1375 and leading into the main priory. With the exception of the tithe barn, it is the only one of the abbey buildings to survive.

Turn down the right-hand edge of the churchyard to reach the tithe barn on your left.

This barn was built as the tithe barn of the abbey. As a feudal landowner, the abbey collected rent or tithes from its tenants, in the form of agricultural produce, some of which was used to feed the canons and lay-brothers, and the rest was sold. These tithes were stored in this huge barn. During the Civil War, Kenilworth Castle was occupied by the Parliamentarians, and saw several skirmishes at the start of the war. Shot marks from those skirmishes can be detected on the walls of the barn.

> **REFRESHMENTS**
>
> The Virgins and Castle pub is just around the corner from the Abbey Fields car park, an interesting old building with outside seating. It offers a good range of beers and food. Telephone: 01926 853737.

Turn left along the wall of the churchyard back to the car park.

HISTORICAL FOOTNOTE

After 1575 Robert Dudley gave up any hopes of marrying the Queen. Instead he secretly married one of her ladies-in-waiting, Lettys Knowles, much to the fury of the Queen when it was discovered. Elizabeth soon forgave Dudley, and was heartbroken when he died in 1588. She outlived him by 15 years, and his last letter to her, found amongst her possessions after her death, had been kept as a treasured memory.

WALK 11
BADDESLEY CLINTON AND THE FORBIDDEN RELIGION

Length: 4 miles

Baddesley Clinton manor house

HOW TO GET THERE: The walk starts from the Kingswood Junction car park entered from Brome Hill Lane, which is off the B4439 in Lapworth.

PARKING: Kingswood Junction car park is clearly signed.

MAP: OS Landranger 139 (GR 186710).

INTRODUCTION

The first part of this walk is along a pleasant stretch of the Grand Union Canal. It then crosses rolling fields to the beautiful moated manor house of Baddesley Clinton, before returning to the start. The walk is on towpaths and field paths, with two short sections of quiet lane. Is has no real gradients, and route-finding is easy.

HISTORICAL BACKGROUND

Although the Catholic faith was banned under Henry VIII, it survived in the Forest of Arden, thanks to the persistence of many local magnates, foremost amongst whom was Henry Ferrers of Baddesley Clinton.

The Reformation divided Europe into two camps ideologically, and religion became a cause of, or at least an element of, many of the conflicts between and within nations. The introduction of the Reformation into England had been primarily for political and dynastic reasons, and both Henry VIII and later his

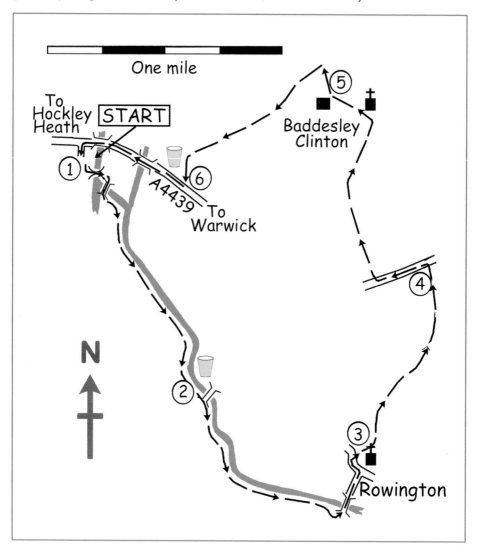

daughter Elizabeth were initially content to accept a public display of loyalty from their subjects whilst turning a blind eye to continued Catholic worship in private. But by the 1570s England had become the foremost of the Protestant countries of northern Europe, and the Catholic Powers, led by Spain, were determined to destabilise the throne prior to replacing Elizabeth with a suitably Catholic monarch. In 1570 Elizabeth was excommunicated by the Pope and her subjects released from loyalty to her. English Catholic priests were trained in Flanders by the exiled cleric William Allen, and from 1574 onwards smuggled back into England to spearhead the old religion. These were joined in 1580 by Jesuit priests, determined to ferment discontent. Catholic writings were printed and spread throughout England to devoted Catholics. English Catholics were openly spoken of by Spain and its allies as tools in their struggle with England.

In response to this, Catholics were subject to increasing repression in England. Very heavy penalties were imposed on those who rejected the Anglican faith, and fines of up to £20 per month were levied for every adult who refused to attend the Anglican church. Catholics were denied public office, and they could not educate their children at public schools. The Ferrers of Baddesley Clinton were devout Catholics, one of a number of eminent local gentry who continued to follow their faith throughout the reign of Elizabeth. Despite the risks involved, they not only continued to celebrate mass in their household chapel, but they also gave refuge to Catholics fleeing persecution, and to Jesuit priests sent from the Continent to maintain the Catholic faith in England. It was the dogged determination of families like the Ferrers that enabled Catholicism to survive in Warwickshire, until more tolerant times returned.

THE WALK

1 From the car park go ahead to the canal basin, seen through the trees. Turn right along the towpath and over a footbridge.

You are crossing the Stratford Canal. This still displays the traditional style of canal building, with narrow locks that can only accommodate one boat at a time. Note also the three inch gap in the centre of the bridge. Barges were originally drawn by horses walking along the towpath, and no provision was made for them to go under bridges. Instead the horse would walk round the top of the bridge and the tow rope would be passed through the gap in the middle. This design can still be seen along the Stratford canal but is rare elsewhere.

Keep ahead, passing to the left of a white cottage, to cross a second footbridge.

Kingswood Junction is where barges could pass between the Stratford Canal (which linked Birmingham with Stratford, the Avon and hence Bristol) and the Grand Union Canal, which connected London with the Midlands and the North.

Turn left and follow the towpath, the canal on your left, to pass under a metal bridge and soon reaching the junction with the Grand Union Canal. Ignore the bridge on your left (No 37) but instead turn right along the canal. Follow the towpath for ¾ mile, to pass under a bridge (No 63), the Tom o'the Wood public house on the opposite bank.

❷   Follow the towpath for another mile to the next bridge (No 62). Leave the canal and cross the bridge. Follow the lane for 250 yards to reach a road. Cross the road, turn left for 5 yards, and then turn right through gates into the churchyard.

❸   Follow the path, keeping to the left of the church, and swinging left past a brick toilet to cross a stile into a field. Keep along the top of the field, the fence close on your left, to cross a stile in the top corner. Turn right down the next field, the hedge close on your right. Keep ahead across a stile into the next field and climb the slope, the hedge still on your right. When the hedge ends, keep ahead to follow a line of trees. Cross the stile and keep ahead down the field to a gate. Keep ahead up the next field, the hedge on your left. When the hedge turns sharp left, keep half left ahead, aiming for a metal gate 200 yards to the right of a red brick house. Go through a kissing gate, 20 yards to the left of the metal field gate. Keep ahead across the next field, hedge close on your right, to reach a gate in the far right-hand corner.

The remains of a windmill can be seen on your left. The building, surrounded by trees, has been converted into a private residence.

❹   Go through the kissing gate and turn left along the lane for 400 yards. About 100 yards past the '40 mph' sign, turn right through a gate and along a green track. Pass a farm on your left and keep ahead along the track, passing through gates and keeping straight on along the hedge-lined track. Follow the track along the edge of a wood. Where the track swings left into fields, keep ahead through a pedestrian gate and keep straight on down the left-hand side of a field. At the end of the field go through a gate, across a narrow field and through a second gate. Keep straight on, to the corner of a fence seen ahead. Follow the fence to a pedestrian gate and then keep ahead along an enclosed footpath. At the end turn sharp left through a gate and follow the drive towards the church. Go through a kissing gate and follow the path through the churchyard, passing the church on your right hand.

The medieval church of St Michael was, like all English churches of that age, initially a Catholic church. The Ferrers, landlords of this manor, worshipped here, together with their tenants. After the Reformation, only Anglican services could be held in it, and instead the family worshipped in their own private chapel in the adjacent Baddesley Clinton House.

Follow the path out through a gate and keep ahead on a path through trees to reach a drive. The entrance to Baddesley Clinton is on your left.

There was a small manor house on this site from at least the early 14th century. Building of the present house was started in the 15th century. It consisted of four ranges of buildings around a central courtyard, with a gatehouse in the eastern range and the whole surrounded by a moat. The Ferrers family bought the house in 1517, and a generation later Henry Ferrers decided to create a far more splendid home for his family. The southern wing was rebuilt and enlarged, the interiors of all the ranges extensively overhauled, with heavy use of wood panelling and overmantles. The western range was demolished in the 18th century.

Henry Ferrers suffered imprisonment for a time, driven into debt by the harsh fines imposed upon him, and rented Baddesley Clinton to two of the daughters of the devoutly Catholic Lord Vaux. During their tenancy the house became a secret meeting place for Jesuit priests, and they employed a master craftsman, Nicholas Owen, to build three priest holes into the house. These were concealed chambers, accessed through hidden panels in the walls or floors, where Catholic priests, together with the paraphernalia of the mass, could be hidden if the house was searched by the authorities. Owen was responsible for constructing secret chambers in many Catholic houses in the area, including Coughton Court (see walk 12). Owen was arrested after the failure of the Gunpowder Plot in 1605 and died under torture, refusing to reveal the location of the many priest holes he had built.

The priest holes were used in 1591, when a conference of Jesuit priests from all over England held at Baddesley Clinton was raided. Although some of the priests slipped away from the house, six were forced to hide for four hours, ankle deep in water in a priest hole hidden in a converted sewer. In 1603 the itinerant Catholic priest Robert Grissold celebrated mass at Baddesley Clinton, and was captured nearby.

In the more tolerant times that followed the Restoration of Charles II in 1660, Baddesley Clinton became headquarters to the Franciscan Fathers of the Second English Province, under Father Leo Randolph, a relative of the Ferrers. Father Leo used the house as the base from which to conduct missions throughout Warwickshire. He also built chapels in nearby Rowington and in Warwick, both of which were destroyed in riots following the deposition of the Catholic monarch, James II.

Baddesley Clinton is open to the public 11 am to 5 pm, Wednesday to Sunday, February to early November; 11 am to 4 pm November until Christmas. There is an entry charge; free to members of National Trust.

⑤ To continue the walk, follow the drive away from the house. Bear left with the drive. Some 200 yards past the bend, just where a parallel drive joins from the left, look for a kissing gate in the fence on the left. Go half left across the ex-deer park, converging with the fence on your left.

The deer park was created by the Ferrers once they bought Baddesley Clinton, an indication of the passion for hunting enjoyed in Tudor England. There are good views back to the house on the left.

Go left around the corner of the fence and then walk to the waymarked gate seen ahead, keeping the fence close on your left hand. Go through the kissing gate and keep ahead, following the tree-lined fence on your left, to go through a gate in the far left-hand corner of the field. Walk quarter-right across the large field, aiming for the red brick building seen on the far side. Go through a gate at the left end of the building, and then half right across the farmyard to a drive. Follow the drive out to a road.

❻ Turn right along the verge for 100 yards to reach the Navigation Inn. Follow the pavement past the pub and over the canal. Continue along the road, passing under a railway bridge and then over a second canal bridge. Just past this bridge, turn left into Brome Hill Lane and walk back to the car park and picnic area.

WALK 12

COUGHTON COURT AND THE GUNPOWDER PLOT OF 1605

Length: 4 miles

The gatehouse at Coughton Court

HOW TO GET THERE: The walk starts from the village green in the centre of Sambourne, 2 miles south of Redditch.

PARKING: There is a lay-by on the village green suitable for parking.

MAP: OS Landranger 150 (GR 061618).

INTRODUCTION

This walk starts in the quiet village of Sambourne before crossing fields to reach Coughton Court. It returns across the typical peaceful Warwickshire countryside of fields, woods and streams. There are no gradients, and route-finding is easy.

HISTORICAL BACKGROUND

Coughton Court has been the home of the Throckmorton family for 600 years, and in 1605 was the backdrop to one of the most memorable events in English history: the Gunpowder Plot.

The accession of James I in 1603 was at first welcomed by English Catholics, who had suffered greatly during Elizabeth's reign (see walk 11). The Throckmortons of Coughton, like many Catholic families, had been financially crippled by the huge fines imposed upon them for non-attendance at the Anglican church, being forced to sell many of their lands to pay them, as well as suffering other persecution. James initially showed considerable toleration of Catholics, relaxing the laws that oppressed them. But in so doing, James raised questions about his own commitment to Protestantism and under pressure from his ministers he was forced to reimpose the former persecution.

Their hopes of a better future dashed, a group of young Catholics devised an audacious plot to murder the King and all his government by blowing up the Houses of Parliament whilst the King was opening the new session. At the same time they would kidnap James's 9-year-old daughter Elizabeth, who would be put on the throne with a Catholic protector. The plot was devised by Robert Catesby, the great-grandson of Sir George Throckmorton, the head of the Throckmorton family. Of the eleven other principal plotters, all but one were from old Catholic families, all but two related in some way to the Throckmortons.

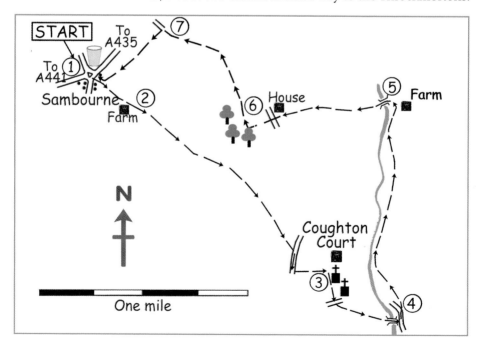

In November 1605 the young Princess Elizabeth was staying at Coombe Abbey, near Coventry. Whilst most of the conspirators were effecting the London end of their scheme, the concurrent plot required an armed party, headed by Sir Everard Digby, to kidnap the princess. Sir George Throckmorton lent Coughton Court to Digby before absenting himself to the Continent, and Digby lived there whilst putting the finishing touches to his plans. On the morning of 5th November, Digby left Coughton to take command of 50 armed men waiting near Coombe Abbey. But then disaster struck. The conspiracy was betrayed by an informer, and Guy Fawkes was dramatically arrested in the cellars of the Palace of Westminster. Some of the plotters, Catesby included, fled northwards to join Digby's group and continue the proposed coup, but what support the plotters had enjoyed faded away once their failure was known. Two days later the last of the plotters were arrested at Holbeach House, near Birmingham.

Whilst Digby's young wife and other sympathizers waited at Coughton for news, the Gunpowder Plot, as it became known to history, ended.

THE WALK

❶ With your back to the Green Dragon, go diagonally across the village green and cross a waymarked drive to the left of the bus shelter. Cross the stile and keep ahead along a green track, at the end of which cross a stile ahead. Keep ahead across the field to cross a stile in the corner ahead. Cross the drive and maintain your direction, keeping the hedge close on your left. Follow the path, now with a wall and soon a barn on your right. Bear right through a gate into a farmyard and then bear left again to resume your previous direction, now along a farm track.

❷ Follow the track past a barn and down to a field gate, at the corner of three fields. Go half left, into the leftmost field, and walk with the hedge close on your right hand. In the field corner, turn left with the boundary, and in 20 yards cross a stile on your right. Resume your previous direction along the next field, the hedge again on your right. At the end of the field cross a stile and keep ahead along the next field, soon crossing a plank bridge and another stile.

Keep ahead along the next field. Cross a stile at the far end and keep ahead, hedge and stream now on your left. Ignore a waymarked footbridge on your left but keep ahead to a gate and then a kissing gate leading onto a road. Cross the road with care to the pavement and then turn right, Coughton Court soon visible on your left. In 200 yards, turn left through a kissing gate into Coughton Park. Keep ahead across the park to a drive. Turn left to the entrance of Coughton Court.

The Warwickshire estate of the de Cocton (or Coughton) family passed through marriage to the Throckmortons in 1409, who came to live on the estate and set about building a far grander house than that already existing. The house, originally surrounded by a moat, was extended and improved throughout the 15th century. In around 1510 the magnificent gatehouse was completed by Sir George Throckmorton. The west front faced out to the surrounding park, and was approached by a bridge over the moat. The east front faced the central courtyard around which the house was built, entry to which is via the large archway in the gatehouse. The arms of the Throckmorton family, an elephant's head over a heraldic casque, can be seen on the outer face, together with the royal coat-of-arms of Henry VIII. It was originally intended that the gatehouse would be free-standing: the wings to either side were built in 1780.

Coughton Court contains a hidden chamber carefully built into its Tower Room, where Catholic priests could be hidden. The Throckmortons had staunchly adhered to the Catholic faith, despite the penalties and persecutions inflicted on them in the Elizabethan period, and had been involved in several plots against the Queen. Edward Arderne of Castle Bromwich was married to Mary Throckmorton, and was executed in 1583 for his part in the Somerville Plot to assassinate Queen Elizabeth. Mary was reprieved and came to live at Coughton, where she was persecuted for 'recusancy', or failure to attend Anglican services. The same year Francis Throckmorton, cousin to the head of the family, Sir George, was executed for his involvement in the plot which bears his name, to replace Elizabeth with her cousin, Mary, Queen of Scots. It was in this gatehouse that in November 1605 Lady Digby anxiously awaited news from her husband. Waiting with her were her young family, two Jesuit priests, the Vaux sisters (relatives of the Throckmortons) and also Nicholas Owen, the man responsible for building priest holes not only at Coughton but at many Catholic houses throughout the Midlands, including Baddesley Clinton (see walk 11).

Coughton Court was badly damaged during the Civil War, and again in 1688, when it was attacked and pillaged by an anti-Catholic mob. A newly-built Catholic chapel in the east wing was burnt down. The Court was finally repaired and rebuilt in 1780, and the moat finally drained in 1795.

Coughton Court is open 11 am to 5 pm, Wednesday to Sunday, mid-March until the end of September, and at weekends throughout October. There is an entrance charge; free to National Trust Members. The car park is administered by the Throckmorton family, and all users are charged.

❸   To continue the walk, go along the drive, away from the Court, soon passing St Peter's church, built by Sir Robert Throckmorton as the family church. Continue along the drive, passing the church of Our Lady and St Joseph. Pass the church and go through the gate to a T-junction of drives. Cross the drive to a kissing gate into a field. Go half left across the field, keeping parallel to the left-hand hedge, to another kissing gate near the left-hand corner of the field. Keep on across the next field, aiming for a gate seen on the far side. Go through the gate and over a footbridge. Turn left along the lane. Follow the lane around a left-hand bend and then immediately turn right through a kissing gate.

④ Climb the bank and then turn left along the field to a kissing gate, visible ahead beside a field gate. Go half right across the next field, crossing a track and converging with trees ahead. Go through a gate and keep ahead across the field, initially with a line of fence posts close on your left, then with a line

of trees on your right. When the trees end, keep ahead to go through a kissing gate. Maintain your direction across the next field to the kissing gate opposite.

Cross a footbridge and keep on across the next field, to cross a footbridge in the left-hand corner and keep ahead across the next field, aiming for a waymark post visible on the far side. Cross another plank bridge and keep ahead through a new plantation to reach the bank of the river Arrow. Keep ahead along the river, passing through a gate and following the bank around to a footbridge.

⑤ Cross the footbridge and then go half right across the field, aiming for an arch in the hedgerow ahead. Keep ahead across the next field, towards a gap in the hedge 100 yards to the right of some trees. Maintain your direction across the next large field, aiming to the left of houses seen ahead. Go through a gate in the top right corner of the field, cross the road to a gateway opposite, then keep ahead along the side of the field, a hedge close on your left.

⑥ On reaching a wood turn right, and walk with the trees on your left. Where the trees end keep ahead at a waymark post and cross the next field, passing an electricity pylon on your right. Keep ahead along the next field, the hedge now on your right. At the far end of the field, cross a stile beside a gate and then immediately turn left onto an enclosed path running along the top edge of the field you have just left. Follow this through a gate onto a concrete drive and immediately turn left over a stile.

⑦ Keep ahead along the edge of a field, a hedge initially on your right. Where the hedge ends keep ahead across the field to cross a footbridge and keep ahead up the next field, aiming for a high hedge ahead. Turn right along the hedge. In 100 yards cross a stile on the left. Follow the clear path across the field to a gate. Cross the corner of the next field to a stile 20 yards ahead. Cross the stile and keep ahead along the green track back to the green at Sambourne.

WALK 13
THE BATTLE OF EDGEHILL 1642

Length: 4 miles

The Warwickshire countryside where the Battle of Edgehill was fought

HOW TO GET THERE: The walk starts from the church in Radway village, 1 mile west of the B4100, 8 miles north of Banbury and 15 miles south of Warwick.

PARKING: There is ample roadside parking in the village.

MAP: OS Landranger 151 (GR 368480).

INTRODUCTION

This walk starts in the attractive village of Radway, and crosses the edge of the battlefield before passing through rolling fields to climb onto the ridge of Edgehill, affording excellent views across the battlefield and the Warwickshire countryside before returning to the village. Route-finding is easy, and there is one short climb to reach the ridge, and one steep descent from it. The second half of the walk can be somewhat overgrown in summer.

HISTORICAL BACKGROUND

In 1642 England lurched into civil war, and the first major battle of that conflict occurred in Warwickshire, at Edgehill.

Ever since the accession of Charles I to the throne in 1625 the country had been slowly sliding towards war, with growing political and religious mistrust set

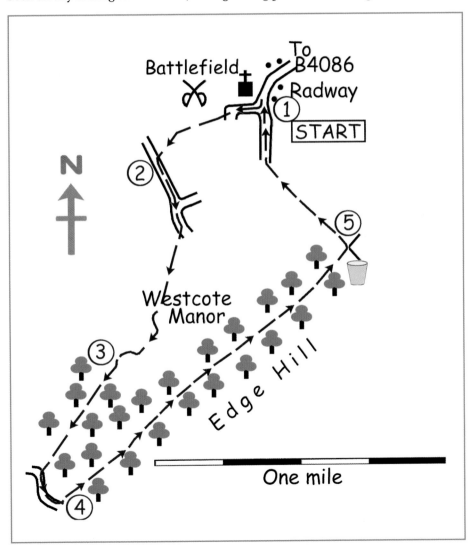

against the background of economic mismanagement. Parliament resented funding government actions over which it had no control, whilst the Catholic king was suspicious of the motives of the Protestant parliament. Parliament's aim was the reform of government, not the removal of the king; the king's aim the preservation of rights he saw as God-given. Posturing, blundering and intransigence on both sides hardened positions, until by the summer of 1642 neither King nor Parliament could see any alternative to armed conflict, and both sides set about raising an army.

England had no standing army, but instead had militia in each county, many inadequately trained, who formed the basis of a national army when required. These were supplemented by additional men raised by local magnates at town or county level. Support for parliament was strongest in the more economically developed areas such as the major cities, the home counties, the Midlands and the West Country. The king's support came from the North and from rural areas. In August 1642 the king raised his standard at Nottingham and started to gather a field army about him, slowly marching towards Shrewsbury and gathering forces all the time. Parliament responded by raising an army in Northampton, under the leadership of the Earl of Essex. By October the king had an army of 14,000 men, Essex one twice that size, but poorly trained and in low morale. After the two armies clashed inconclusively near Worcester, the king turned and marched towards London, aiming to end the war at a stroke. Essex did likewise, aiming to keep the king from entering the capital.

Both armies were hampered by large baggage trains and cumbersome artillery, and made slow progress, foraging for supplies as they went. Neither had any system for intelligence gathering, and both were only faintly aware of the location of their opponent. On 22nd October the king rested his army at Edgecote, near Banbury, whilst the Parliamentarian army camped a mere 7 miles away at Kineton. Neither side realised the other was that close until their foragers ran into one another. After debating whether to make a run for London, the king decided to turn and fight. The battle of Edgehill was at hand.

THE WALK

❶   With your back to the lych gate leading into the church, turn right along the lane. In a few yards bear right into Tysoe Road. Turn left with the lane and in 100 yards go through a gate on your right.

Look to your left. The ridge of Edgehill stands 300 ft above you, looking very different today to how it looked in 1642. Then the ridge was largely treeless, with isolated clumps of shrubs on its slopes. There were no buildings on the ridge: the turret you see is the Castle Inn, built at the end of the 19th century. The king took the decision to turn and fight on the evening of 22nd October, but because his forces were scattered in camps and billets across several square miles it was not until midday on the 23rd that his army was reassembled and marched back to meet the Parliamentarians. The Royalist infantry scrambled down the ridge you are looking at and lined up in battle order just behind you. The cavalry, in two wings, made their way down the gentler ends of the ridge.

Go half left across the field to pass through a metal pedestrian gate and maintain your direction across the corner of the field to a second pedestrian gate. Go half left across the next field to another pedestrian gate beside a field gate, then pause and look to your right, to the fence and beyond.

The Royalist army lined up on your right, just beyond where the fence now stands. The Royalist infantry were drawn up in five brigades, two to the rear (immediately to your right as you stand and look at the fence) and three brigades in front of them (you are behind the left end of that front line). Each brigade was comprised of approximately 2,200 men, divided equally between musketeers and pikemen. The musketeers were armed with cumbersome 4½ ft-long muzzle-loading muskets, capable of killing at a range of 50-100 yards, but which took a minute to reload after each firing. During that minute the musketeers were vulnerable to attack, and so they were protected by pikemen armed with 14 ft-long double-edged pikes. Cannon were placed between the brigades. The Royalist cavalry were lined up on the two wings of the army, 1,000 on the left wing under Lord Wilmot, and 1,700 under Prince Rupert on the right wing. In all the Royalist army was 14,000-15,000 strong.

Although the Parliamentarian army had been over 25,000 strong at Worcester, its commander the Earl of Essex had been leaving garrisons along his line of march, and by the time he reached Edgehill he also had about 15,000 men. These were drawn up facing the Royalists, a mile down the slope towards Kineton. They too had two lines of infantry brigades, with cavalry on both wings. The major difference was in the ratio of pikes to muskets, the Parliamentarian army having the more conventional ratio of one pikeman for every two musketeers, rather than the 1:1 ratio in the Royalist army.

It was not until mid-afternoon on 23rd October that the two armies were lined up and ready to fight. For the Earl of Essex, there was little incentive to open hostilities. He was in the weaker position, downhill from his enemy and needing to advance up a reasonable slope in the face of enemy fire. He was also well aware that reinforcements were on their way to him, as the garrisons he had left behind marched rapidly to join him. A third consideration was that in this, the first armed conflict between Parliament and the King, it was in Parliament's interests for the King to initiate the battle, enabling Parliament to paint him as the aggressor. At 3 pm, after addressing his troops, King Charles gave the order for battle to commence.

Keep ahead across the next field, parallel to a fence on your right, to a gate into a lane.

This lane existed in 1642, and the leftmost of the Royalist infantry brigades stood just beyond the sharp bend to your right. On the other side of the lane was a network of small fields and enclosures, and it was in these that the left wing of Royalist cavalry under Lord Wilmot was deployed. In front of them a screen of musketeers and light horsemen faced a similar Parliamentarian force.

② Turn left along the lane. Where the lane bends left, keep ahead along King Johns Lane. In 100 yards, opposite a house and just before the lane bends left, turn right through a gate. Walk half left across a field, aiming for an apparent gap in the hedge on the far side of the field. Go through a kissing gate and then half left up the next field, to go through a field gate. Maintain your direction, aiming for houses at the top of the field. Go through a field gate, then half right to the corner of the fence ahead before resuming your previous direction, the fence now close on your left hand.

Where the fence turns left, turn left and go up the field to a kissing gate. Turn right along a tarmac track for 50 yards. At the junction of tracks, go right through a green metal pedestrian gate, and immediately turn left to walk along the top of the field, the fence close on your left. Pass Westcote Manor.

③ Continue ahead into woods. Follow the path through the woods for ½ mile, maintaining your direction to eventually reach a road. Turn left and follow the road up a steep hill.

This road follows the gentler slope around the flank of Edgehill, and it was down this slope that Wilmot's cavalry made their way to reach their battle positions.

At the top of the hill the road bends left, with a house on your right. Opposite the house turn left onto a path into trees.

④ Follow the wooded path along the top of the slope for ½ mile. On reaching a tarmac drive turn left downhill for 100 yards, then take the waymarked path on your right. Follow this woodland path along the top of the ridge for another ½ mile. At a cross-track turn left, and 10 yards later fork right onto the uppermost path. In another 500 yards you come to another cross-track. To visit the Castle Inn, turn right uphill. To continue the walk, turn left down to a kissing gate.

From the kissing gate there is a superb view over the battlefield of Edgehill. Today the landscape is broken up with hedgerows and stands of trees, but in 1642 it was very different. In front of Radway church, seen in front of you, was a wide unbroken plain stretching down to Kineton 3 miles away. The Royalist infantry were lined up just beyond the church, the Parliamentarians facing them a mile beyond that (the buildings of the modern army depot mark roughly the spot). On your left the line of King Johns Lane can be seen, and beyond that were the enclosures and small fields where Wilmot's cavalry were deployed. Round to your right is the line of the modern B4086, and it was here that the Royalist right-wing cavalry, under the command of the

King's nephew Prince Rupert, were deployed, facing their Parliamentarian counterparts.

After a desultory exchange of artillery fire, the two wings of Royalist cavalry charged forward, routing the Parliamentarian horse, who fled back into their infantry lines, hotly pursued. These infantry ranks then broke and retreated in disorder, chased by the Royalist cavalry who pursued with such enthusiasm that they rode entirely off the battlefield and played no further part in the action. The Royalist infantry advanced, pushing with pike at the Parliamentarian centre, but failing to break through. The shattered Parliamentarian wings and the remnants of their cavalry then reformed, and pushed the Royalists back. As the early October night fell, the battle petered out in confusion and exhaustion. The Royalist army struggled back up the slope in front of you, whilst the Parliamentarians regrouped around Kineton. Three thousand men were left dead or wounded on the field.

5 Go through the kissing gate and down the field, a fence close on your right.

The obelisk visible in the field on your right was erected in the 19th century to commemorate the battle. Its location has no historical significance.

At the bottom of the field, keep ahead through a kissing gate and continue along the next field, the fence close on your left. At the end go through a kissing gate and keep ahead through a field gate. Follow the drive out to a lane at a pond and turn right. Follow the lane back to the T-junction in front of the church.

HISTORICAL FOOTNOTE

After the battle of Edgehill, King Charles marched to Oxford and from thence towards London. The Earl of Essex, his army reinforced by his garrisons, marched directly to the capital, arriving before the king and blocking his approach. The king retreated, and the capital was never again seriously threatened by the Royalists. Both sides claimed Edgehill as a victory. In reality, the battle itself was inconclusive, but Essex achieved his goal of delaying the king's advance on London. A decisive victory for either side at Edgehill could well have been the knockout blow that ended the Civil War before it really began. Instead, the war was to continue for another seven years, costing the lives of many thousands more, including, ultimately, the king himself.

WALK 14

HATTON FLIGHT AND THE
TRANSPORT REVOLUTION

Length: 4 miles

The impressive Hatton flight of locks

HOW TO GET THERE: The walk starts from the Hatton Locks car park, signposted off the A4177 Warwick to Solihull road, 2 miles out of Warwick, and 100 yards short of the Waterman public house.

PARKING: In the Hatton Locks pay-and-display car park.

MAP: OS Landranger 151 (GR 242669).

INTRODUCTION

From Hatton this walk follows the Grand Union Canal down the spectacular Hatton Flight, before returning across the fields, passing through an interesting churchyard at Budbrooke. The walk is on towpaths, field paths and a quiet lane. It is easy underfoot and route-finding is simple.

HISTORICAL BACKGROUND

The late 18th century was the era of the Transport Revolution, when canals were built the length and breadth of England. Spectacular feats of engineering were required, and there are few better examples than the series of locks known as the Hatton Flight.

For the Industrial Revolution to succeed, it was necessary for there to be a corresponding revolution in transport. The large-scale production of goods needed not only new technology and new ways of organising labour, but also the means to move increasing quantities of raw materials and finished goods quickly and cheaply around the country. In the mid-18th century these means did not exist apart from around the coast. Rivers were often obstructed by weirs and fishpools, and very few could provide for the long-distance haulage of goods. Roads were of very poor quality, rutted and unsurfaced. Although the growth of the turnpikes – essentially private toll roads reasonably well maintained – improved the situation for passenger traffic, they were unsuitable for moving large volumes of goods. In Derbyshire freight transport still relied upon the packhorse, up to a hundred animals in a line, carrying goods slowly and laboriously along narrow tracks.

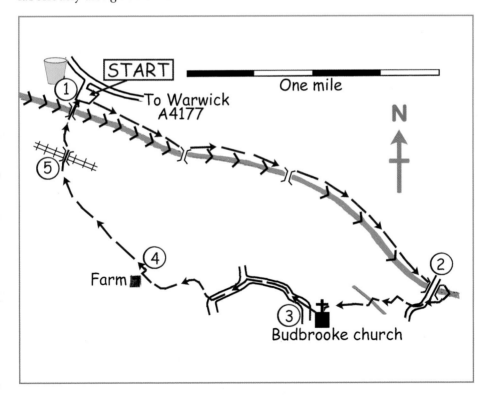

In 1759 a revolution in transport occurred. Francis Egerton, 2nd Duke of Bridgewater, tired of London society and disappointed in love, threw his energies into constructing a canal to connect his coalmines in Worsley to nearby Manchester. To do this Bridgewater employed James Brindley, a millwright with no formal education, who brought a natural genius to the task of civil engineering, overcame tremendous natural obstacles, and in 1761 opened the first commercial canal in England.

The success of the canal as a means of moving heavy goods quickly and cheaply was immediately apparent, and the next 60 years saw canals being opened in such numbers that it was described as 'canal mania'. Birmingham, which grew into Britain's foremost industrial town, became the hub of a nationwide network of canals, necessary to import raw materials into the city and export finished goods. But there were major obstacles to bringing canals to Birmingham, primarily the town's situation on top of a plateau. The canal builders needed to show considerable ingenuity, building long flights of locks, of which the most spectacular can be seen at Hatton.

THE WALK

❶ From the car park, keep ahead to the canal and turn left down the towpath.

The canal network grew piecemeal with, for instance, four separate canals all in competition with one another, being built into Birmingham between 1769 and 1793. However, James Brindley, rightly viewed as the father of the canals, had a vision of a unified canal system that would link all of England. So was born the idea of the Grand Union Canal, which you are walking beside now. Brindley set out to link existing canals into one huge network, building connections where necessary and upgrading the existing canals to a uniform standard. By 1783 Birmingham had been connected to London, but by a very circuitous route through Coventry and Rugby. A more direct route would be a canal through Warwick, but this would have to drop from the Birmingham plateau down its steepest slope. This necessitated a large number of locks. Many were individual locks, but in places several locks occurred together in what is known as a flight. One such flight, made up of five locks, is a few miles uphill at Knowle (see walk 4), but here at Hatton the slope was so steep that it necessitated 21 locks in less than 2 miles. Known as the 'Steps to Heaven', this is one of the longest flights of locks in the country, and it takes four hours for boats to traverse them. With the completion of Hatton Flight the Grand Union between Birmingham and Warwick was opened in 1800.

Follow the towpath for 1½ miles to reach bridge 50C.

As you walk down the canal you will see a number of large bays and pools of water alongside the canal. These acted as reservoirs: 21 locks release an enormous amount of water as a barge travels downstream. The solution to this was to have pumping stations at the bottom of long flights of locks, and to pump the water from the bottom back up to the top. A pumping station was built 4 miles downstream from here, in the flat countryside beyond Leamington, and the water moved back to beyond the top of the flight. Reservoirs were created down its length to further retain water in the system.

Note also the width and length of the locks. In the earlier canals, locks were wide enough to accommodate one barge at a time, and frequently only long enough for one. When Brindley designed the Grand Union he improved the locks, making them wide enough for two barges and often lengthening them to accommodate two more, thus greatly increasing the rate at which barges could move up and down the canal.

② The walk now crosses the canal. Go under bridge 50C to the white-painted Hatton Bottom Lock cottage and then turn right across the lock gates to the car park on the far side. (If you have any trepidation about crossing the lock, this can be avoided by turning left up a footpath immediately before bridge 50C, and then turning right along the road to rejoin the walk at the traffic lights.) Keep ahead across the car park to the access road and turn right to reach the main road. Cross the road and turn left along the pavement for 50 yards to reach traffic lights (the alternative route rejoins here).

Turn right immediately before the traffic lights along a footpath. In 10 yards cross a stile and keep ahead, the access road to the car parks on your immediate left. In 30 yards, just before the entrance to the car parks, turn right over a footbridge. Keep ahead, the fence on your left. Cross a stile and enter a field. Immediately turn left to walk along the field boundary, the fence still on your left. Turn right in the field corner and continue along the field boundary, an embankment now on your left. In the next corner turn left through an arch beneath the railway. Go through the gate ahead and then head half-right across the field, aiming 100 yards to the right of the church tower. Go through a kissing gate in the corner of hedges and then keep ahead to another kissing gate seen on the far side of the field. Go through into the churchyard and keep ahead to reach a paved path.

This church was built initially to serve the small community of Budbrooke. It saw additional service when the Royal Warwickshire Regiment built its main barracks at Budbrooke, and the church was used by the regiment, both for services and as a graveyard. Note the double rows of small iron crosses that line the grassy path you are walking along. These commemorate members of the Royal Warwickshire who are buried here.

③ Turn right along the path to a gate leading into a lane and turn right. Follow the lane for 700 yards. Where the lane bends right, turn left along a side road, signed 'Hatton on the Hill'. In 200 yards, where the lane bends left, turn right along an unsurfaced track and follow it to a farm. Pass the entrance to barns on the left and, 30 yards later, where the track turns left into the farmyard, turn right.

REFRESHMENTS

The Waterman public house stands on the hillside at the start of the walk, with a beer garden and a terrace affording fine views of Hatton Flight. It has a range of food and beers. Telephone: 01926 492427.

❹ Go through a metal gate and immediately turn left through a second gate. Keep straight ahead up the side of a field, a fence initially on your left, to go through a kissing gate ahead of you, leading into a second field. Go half right down the field. A waymarked kissing gate comes into view in the bottom of the field. Go over a footbridge and up steps into the next field. Keep ahead along a clear path over the field and then through a gap in the hedge into another field. Maintain your direction across this field, aiming for a green metal bridge seen on the far side.

❺ Cross the bridge over the railway and then bear right into a field and walk on, initially with trees and hedgerow on your right. Where the hedge ends, keep ahead over the open field to a kissing gate seen to the left of buildings ahead. Go through the kissing gate and up steps, then keep ahead across the bridge back to the car park and the start.

If you turn left up the towpath for a few yards you will pass a number of relics of the golden age of canals, including models of the dock mechanism and a dredger barge.

As you pass over the bridge, look to your right. There is a lock, no longer in use, that is still the original narrow gauge of lock-gate. Gates of this width were all upgraded to double-width gated along the Grand Union, but remained in use on other canals. Examples can be seen on the Stratford Canal (see walk 2). This narrow gauge lock was converted into a dry dock, used for repairing barges.

To visit the Waterman pub, go through a kissing gate to the left of the white-painted Hatton Dry Dock building and keep up the field to the pub.